Retirement Roulette

ARE YOU PUTTING YOUR RETIREMENT ON THE LINE?

J. Mark Truttman

Platinum Retirement Solutions
DUBLIN, CALIFORNIA
CA LICENSE NO. 0B06466

J. Mark Truttman/Platinum Retirement Solutions
6379 Clark Ave, Suite 220
Dublin, CA 94568
www.platinumretirementsolutions.com

Book layout ©2013 BookDesignTemplates.com

Retirement Roulette/ J. Mark Truttman. —1st ed.
ISBN 9781791593476

Contents

CHAPTER 1

You're Not a Kid Anymore

This is going to come off as something close to blasphemy to some of my friends in the financial services industry. I'll say it anyway:

Given the financial products available today for either pre-retired or retired people, I believe there is absolutely no reason to take losses by exposing themselves completely to the roller coaster ride of the stock market.

No, that's not something you will hear from the typical financial professional.

But I've never been that guy, as you will quickly see in this book. I'm someone who had little opportunity to take risks, someone who had to start fending for myself early when I was all but on my own well before my high school graduation. My conservative approach to growing and protecting money developed at a time when I had to be careful with every dollar I earned and how it was spent.

It's the same approach I use today in helping clients of Platinum Retirement Solutions grow and protect their money.

Please don't misunderstand me. I'm not saying that people wise enough to save and invest in their own futures should never take the risks inherent in any investment tied directly to the stock market. Far from it. "No risk, no reward" is an adage one can live with at certain times of life.

Much younger times, that is. The years immediately approaching retirement, however, are not those times.

We go through our life in different phases — the growth and the accumulation phase, then the conservation and distribution phase — as it relates to our money. The first phase is the time to be focused on the growth of your money, and that's done by a younger crowd — people 35, 40, 45, even 50 years of age. But people approaching retirement at age 55 or 60 need to start thinking differently about conservation and the ultimate distribution of that money. In short, this is the time to harvest the crop they planted and cultivated. It is the time to turn assets into the income that will be essential for the remainder of their lives.

> *It's been my experience in working for nearly 25 years primarily with people preparing for or already in retirement that they are far more interested in protecting what they have earned in life than they are in increasing what they might make after they've stopped working.*

We do a lot of risky things as kids. We race cars on the street, drive when we shouldn't, drink cheap wine, jump into swimming pools from second-story balconies of spring-break motels. These are things we wouldn't even think of doing when we grow older and get smart enough to realize we now break more easily and don't mend as quickly as we once did.

The same thing holds true for folks nearing retirement who speculate in the stock market with money they can't afford to lose. That's why I really can't believe it when I see people already in retirement taking substantial losses during inevitable market downturns. They have retired, their earning power isn't what it was when they were working and they're out of time to recover what they just lost.

Yet, some still live in a dream world where, after they take a big loss in the market, they believe things will turn around in a week, a month, or six months. They're playing the game the same way they did as a much younger investor. Well, I don't own a crystal ball, so I can't forecast when a down market will rebound, though it usually does. But I can play devil's advocate and ask this question:

Why wouldn't those same folks look at the crazy rises and falls of the stock market and say, "You know what, I'm done with this game. I'm tired of paying people to lose my money. It's time to protect what I have, accept conservative but reasonable growth, take the income to live the way I want to live and then make sure I can pass on to my family whatever I don't spend in life."

It's been my experience in working for nearly 25 years primarily with people preparing for or already in retirement that they are far more interested in protecting what they have earned in life than they are in increasing what they might make after they've stopped working. We're going to talk throughout this book about established ways to both protect and grow retirement money. "Retirement money," you must understand, is money that can't be allowed to slip away. That makes it different from "investment money," which you can reasonably afford to expose to some risk in the hope of getting a better reward.

Retirement money is the foundation of income upon which your retirement dreams are built. It consists of Social Security, payments from a defined-benefit pension (if you're still lucky enough to have one of those), and money you've saved and invested that grows most typically in tax-deferred pools such as the individual retirement account (IRA), a 401(k), 403(b) or any other qualified or non-qualified retirement accounts.

But any foundation can crack. That is more likely to happen to folks who continue to gamble with retirement money they can't afford to lose by exposing too much to the ever-changing winds of the stock market. That's hard for me to watch, especially when there are other ways to avoid the risk and still grow your money.

The Lost Decade

The first decade of this century brought dramatic evidence of what can happen when riding the winds of Wall Street.

The dot-com boom of 1999, when the technology-heavy NASDAQ index rose more than 85 percent — suddenly became the dot-com bust of 2000 through 2002 as the NASDAQ fell 39, 21 and 31 percent, respectively. The S&P 500, a broader reflection of the overall market, had a similar downturn with less dramatic but still significant tumbles of 10, 13 and 23 percent in those three years.

Things recovered over time, as they usually do, with the NASDAQ getting a 50 percent bump in 2003, the year the S&P 500 rose 26 percent. The market stayed in the black for the next three years, though with only 3 percent growth in 2005.

The bottom fell out again, however, with the bursting of the sub-prime mortgage bubble in the late fall of 2007.

The S&P 500 limped to the finish line that year with a 3.5 percent gain before falling a devastating 38.5 percent in 2008. The Dow Jones Industrial Average bottomed out on March 9, 2009 at a 12-year-low of 6,547 after setting a then-record of 14,164 as recently as Oct. 9, 2007. Before the country's greatest economic downturn since the Great Depression was declared officially over in June 2009, the average U.S. worker in 2008 saw his 401(k) lose more than 24 percent, and accounts with more than $200,000 lost even more, on average.[1]

To be sure, many investors who were years from needing retirement income eventually recovered their losses, though it took several years. Imagine, though, the impact on those who were actively taking income streams from their market-based retirement accounts in 2008.

> *Sure, some people can handle that wild ride. Good for them. But remember, it's where you are in your life that should determine whether you take the ride or stay off.*

Let's consider the example of a man taking 5 percent a year out of his $500,000 IRA account — $25,000 — to supplement his Social Security income and any capital gains he may have on investments. A rule of thumb in investment distribution says a typical investor can safely afford to take out 4 percent annually, the theory being that a typical stock market return will more than replace the withdrawn amount.

Just the opposite happened in 2008. If the man in our example lost 25 percent of his half-million-dollar account that year as many people did, his account lost $125,000 and he's now taking 5 percent of $375,000. That means he's receiving only $18,750 instead of the

---

[1] Lauren Young. Bloomberg. Oct. 5, 2009. "Typical U.S. Worker Saw 401(k) Lose 24.3% in 2008." https://www.bloomberg.com/news/articles/2009-10-05/typical-u-dot-s-dot-worker-saw-401-k-lose-24-dot-3-percent-in-2008.

$25,000 he took a year earlier. Remember, too, that his account value decreases with each withdrawal.

Let me put it bluntly here: I don't care who you are or how much money you have, if you're living off a pool of money that's tied to the whims of the stock market, you will from time to time lose money you can't afford to lose. Eventually as your account value diminishes, you will begin to worry about running out of money — the No. 1 fear of most retired people. You may have thought you were living the life of Riley, but you may suddenly find you can no longer live that same lifestyle.

Why Take the Risk?

And so, I ask the question again: Why would you even want to take that kind of chance with your retirement foundation savings when there are other ways to protect your principal, to have a moderate but steady growth potential in your account values, and guarantee yourself a source of lifetime income that you cannot outlive?

No doubt some readers will have guessed by now that I am talking here about insurance-based products — the only tools available that can do all the things described in the paragraph above.

Yeah, I know what you're thinking. Products such as life insurance and annuities are dirty words to some people nearing or having entered into retirement. "Why do I need life insurance at my age?", they ask, reasonably. Or, "I've heard a lot of concerns about annuities, especially the fee structure. People tell me they aren't the way to go."

Well, as someone who fervently believes that steady, guaranteed protection and growth is the most important component of retirement income, I'm writing this book in part to encourage a change in mindset, a paradigm shift people need to consider when it comes to growing and protecting the money they can't afford to lose from the shifting winds that swirl through Wall Street.

Sure, some people can handle that wild ride. Good for them. But remember, it's where you are in your life that should determine whether you take the ride or stay off.

It's why I believe strongly in the value of insurance-based products. Simply put, only insurance companies — which have protected consumers over the trials of time with pillars that include maintaining required legal reserves, and which are subject to strict regulation in each state — have the ability to provide products that guarantee principal, provide competitive interest rates, provide both death and living benefits, and provide a stream of lifetime income that will not fall off if and when markets do.

We'll discuss some of those products in detail later in this book. We'll talk about fixed indexed universal life insurance policies that provide death benefits for your heirs, living benefits for the insured that include provisions for long-term care, protection of your principal, and are positioned to Earn interest tied to the movement of an external market index without ever being invested in the market itself. We'll talk about indexed annuities, that offer a more modest but guaranteed interest rate while insuring against loss of principal.

We'll talk about preparing an income strategy and how that differs in varying stages of life. We'll talk about ways to help taxes using Roth conversion strategies. We'll talk about the role that life insurance products play when passing benefits on to heirs, as well as their potential to create a tax-free income source and long-term care benefits.[2]

---

[2] Policy loans and withdrawals will reduce available cash values and death benefits, and may cause the policy to lapse or affect any guarantees against lapse. Additional premium payments may be required to keep the policy in force. In the event of a lapse, outstanding policy loans in excess of unrecovered cost basis will be subject to ordinary income tax. Tax laws are subject to change. You should consult a tax professional.

We'll talk, in short, about taking the kind of steady and safe approach to making sure you have positioned yourself to enjoy a lifetime income stream that survives any whims of the stock market. Not only is this the smart approach, it's an absolute must.

I've said this many times to clients and prospective clients, some of whom didn't necessarily like what I had to tell them. I'm not the guy to make you rich. I'm not going to suggest that or even imply it. But, I am going to help you make the best use of the assets you have, so they can work in the best way for you over time.

CHAPTER 2

Can You Handle the Truth?

I would love to share nothing but happy stories in this book, though sadly that will not always be the case.

I've got plenty to tell, mind you, about clients who had the foresight to do their retirement planning right. These are people who had the insight to realize they needed to start something early and begin growing their nest egg by saving whatever they could — most likely a little more than a lot — as soon as they could. They added on when their personal finances improved as their careers did, or as opportunities such as inheritances came along. With some modifications as they neared retirement — transitioning from the accumulation phase to the conservation and distribution phase — these people with foresight will enter their nonworking years knowing they did the best they could to put themselves in position to retire confidently.

I truly love helping people, and in 25 years of working in retirement planning I've seen some fabulous success stories — some of which ended well despite a rocky start.

Truly, many don't know how well they've done — or how much better than can do with some adjustments — until you break it down with them.

I'm especially fond of one involving a real guy to whom I'll assign a fictitious name.

Ted was a Vietnam veteran in his 50s who, because of contact with Agent Orange and other chemicals the troops used in fighting the Southeast Asia war, had a history of joint problems that eventually left him unable to work. When I first met him, he had been turned down in his attempt to get Social Security disability. He was also having trouble getting benefits from the Department of Veterans Affairs.

Even though I had nothing to gain financially from helping Ted with his disability issue, I set him up with someone I knew who was an expert in that field. Ted soon got the disability help he needed and, after a few years, he and his wife moved into a home they loved out in the country south of San Jose.

Eventually, I began working with Ted to develop a strategy to provide lifetime income for himself and his wife.

I'm delighted to say, a few years after we began restructuring some things, Ted and his wife came to tell me they had bought a piece of land in northern California and had built the house of their dreams there. Better yet, after selling his house in south San Jose, he hadn't needed to take out any loans to pay the contractors and builders on the project north of the Bay.

Bottom line, Ted didn't get greedy with what money he had. He didn't play it overly safe, but he used various strategies, which included annuities, to grow that money through a fixed index annuity, which provided him interest tied to an external market index, while avoiding the risk of losing his principal. He's now receiving income from the income provided by the income riders of these annuities — aspects of annuities we will discuss in Chapter 5.

His is the kind of success story that makes me feel good about what I do. Here was a guy not in a good situation, but I was able to help him in part by showing him and his wife how to grow their money and build an income strategy that included steady, conservative financial vehicles. They now know exactly where their money is coming from and at what stages of their lives they can expect it. They also have optional features on their annuities in place to trigger income over time to compensate for inflation.

They're in a nice place.

To me, they illustrate what can happen when people don't fall victim to greed. When they instead become more like "The Little Engine That Could," the children's fable that makes a valid point about the great things that can be accomplished with slow, steady progress coupled with determination and discipline.

You May Not Want to Hear This, But ...

I've also seen some real disasters.

These usually become apparent during an early meeting, a session I call "getting financially naked" in which we take a detailed look at exactly where a prospective client stands in their retirement approach. Let's be candid here: If you don't have a realistic picture of where you are today, you can't expect to envision where you can be in the future.

We begin this fact-finding process with a triage of income and expenses. We prepare a monthly budget covering all likely expenses — mortgage/rent payments, home and car insurance, taxes, utilities, outstanding loans, groceries, clothing, entertainment/hobbies, dining out, vacation/travel, gas and auto repairs, health insurance, life insurance, recurring medical costs, vet bills, credit card bills, alimony payments, etc.

Against that monthly budget estimate, we project anticipated monthly retirement income from sources that could include Social Security, pension, retirement plans such as IRAs and 401(k)s, personal savings, and dividends and capital gains from investments.

In the end, the financial picture we develop sometimes looks better than expected for many people who looked ahead and prepared for their retirement years. Truly, many don't know how well they've done — or how much better than can do with some adjustments — until you break it down with them.

For too many other people, sadly, the picture looks pretty bleak.

One such couple came to see me in response to one of my radio shows. He was 54, she was 51. They had a couple of young-adult children — one in college, one about to be. The husband was the only one bringing in substantial income, though the wife had a part-time job as a personal trainer.

They had the same concerns many people do: "Am I going to have enough money to live on in retirement? What do I need to do to get to the milestones I set for myself?" The majority of their retirement fund was inheritance from his parents, part of a qualified IRA on which he was paying a truckload of taxes as he took out big chunks to pay for his kids' tuition. The guy was routinely putting in 14-hour days, busting his butt to make it all work.

They were sitting across the table from me — she was looking Barbie-doll pretty in her workout suit while he sat with his head in his hands looking miserable. We did an analysis on how much money was coming in and how much was going out, and we quickly developed a picture of where they were and where they might be.

"What do you think we need to do?" she asked.

"You need to get a job," I answered as honestly as I could.

She seemed floored that I had the audacity to even suggest she go to work. He took the news worse than she did. His hands on his forehead, his elbows on his knees, I thought he was about to cry.

What are we looking for as we prepare for retirement: definitive numbers that we can control, or a mirage?

What was I supposed to tell them? It was clear he was breaking his neck to pay the bills while she seemed content with the status quo. The kids didn't have any college scholarships, and worse yet, they weren't applying for any. Why not? Even small scholarships add up to help buy books and pay fees.

Instead, everything was falling on Dad, who felt the pressure to take everything on his shoulders. They were all but killing the guy! Their numbers didn't lie. With what they were spending and what they were making, they were actually going backward in gross assets.

It was almost as if they needed a financial intervention. What they did after leaving me I don't know — I never heard from them again. I might have been able to help them address their problem, but it was going to require putting some discipline in their finances that they weren't willing to accept just yet.

How Did I Get in This Hole?

At the same time, I understand how people fall into this situation.

When we're younger, we don't think about this stuff. We need most of what we earn to start families, pay the rent or buy a first home, maybe pay off student loans. We're more intent on a career path than a road to retirement. Such is the cycle of life.

Then the kids come along, and now there are even more regular expenses. You're probably going to need a bigger house, and it's at this time that really thoughtful people begin thinking about saving for college educations.

And then one day you're 45, 50 years old and suddenly you start thinking, "You know what? I'm running out of time. I'm 50 and I've got only another 15, 16 years of working and putting away enough money to live on for the rest of my life. How am I going to do that in the working years I have left?"

For many people, this is the first time they come to see a retirement professional such as myself. Sadly for some of them, the picture they see when looking into their future — based on their financial situation of today — is a kick in the butt.

I don't like having to show people that picture. But all I can do is tell them the truth, which is what you're going to hear from me. I believe that too many people in my business offer smoke and mirrors.

They sugarcoat things and tell people what they want to hear — that everything is going to be OK. But is it? What are we looking for as we prepare for retirement: definitive numbers that we can control, or a mirage?

Different Needs at Different Times

Fortunately, a lot of people do get it and start planning for their retirement well in advance.

They understand retirement is a long-term venture. They recognize that, when they retire at whatever age, they can hope to live a long time because of advances in medicine, healthy eating and a healthier lifestyle. They might live 30, 35 years after retirement.

The question even good planners have to ask is, "If I live that long, where is my paycheck going to come from?"

Talking about ways to keep getting that paycheck is a big part of what we do as insurance and income professionals at Platinum Retirement Solutions.

Our approach, the specifics of which we will detail in later chapters, makes us a bit different from the financial professional who might have served you well in a different phase of your life. But the professional you worked with in your 30s and 40s — when you toiled hard to grow your money in the risk/reward world of market-based investments — may not be the best person to guide you into the years of protecting and ultimately taking income from those assets you've worked so hard to accumulate.

That's why I tell prospective clients it's important to get with the right professional at different phases of your life.

If you're 35 and in the accumulation phase of life, you may have been told to be concerned primarily with investing and saving. This is the time of life when you can likely afford to deal with the ups and downs of stocks, bonds, exchange-traded funds and other market-related investments.

It all comes down to having the right guide at the right time of your life.

At the same time, however, it's never too early to start thinking about life insurance. That's especially the case with today's products, which provide not only the traditional death-benefit protection for a still-young family, but also offer the potential for cash value growth that can be used later in life as a tax-free income stream to supplement your retirement income. In an era where nothing about Social Security can be taken for granted, that alternative source of income is something a 35-year-old in the 21st century should consider.

It's also never too late to start thinking about the income-generating prospects of life insurance.

In the upcoming Chapter 7 on the life insurance products of today, we'll talk about how people 55-and-older can use life insurance not only for its legacy purposes, but also as a means of maximizing tax-free income in retirement. We'll also talk about how people even older than that can use life insurance as a way of defraying some of the tax hit they will incur upon taking required minimum distributions, or RMDs, at age 70½ from tax-deferred retirement accounts such as IRAs and 401(k)s.

It all comes down to having the right guide at the right time of your life.

Just as you wouldn't ask your barber to fix your teeth — not since the Middle Ages, anyway — nor should you expect the financial representative who helped you invest your money for growth may not be the same person who helps you make a transition into making sure your portfolio can guarantee you income for life, income not subject to the volatility of the stock market.

To get started on being realistic with your own finances, take stock of your answers on the following worksheet.

	Your Monthly Expenses (aka: Budget)					
Housing	Rent/mortgage		**Transportation**	Public transit	
	Home insurance			Gas	
	Utilities			Parking/tolls	
	Internet/cable			Maintenance	
	Phones			Insurance	
	Taxes			Loan payments	
	Household supplies			Other	
	Total	$		**Total**	$
Food	Groceries		**Personal**	Child care	
	Meals out			Gifts	
	Other			Clothes/shoes	
	Total	$		Laundry	
Health	Medicine			Donations	
	Insurance			Entertain-ment	
	Out-of-pocket			Beauty care	
	Other			Other	
	Total	$		**Total**	$
Finance	Financial professional		**Other**	School costs	
	Bank fees			Credit cards	
	Other fees/ expenses			Savings	
	Total	$		**Total**	$
				Grand Total	$

CHAPTER 3

Hard Lessons Learned Early

The lady of leisure I described in the previous chapter — the one in the workout suit who seemed shocked when I told her she would have to get a job in order to meet her and her husband's retirement goals — probably thought I was being pretty tough on her.

She's right. I'm a little rough about the edges, and I know this. So be it.

I tend to be a brutally honest person when it comes to helping people do the things they've simply got to do in order to meet the financial needs or retirement goals they set for themselves. I can live with that. I've been living that way — out of necessity — all of my life.

I'll not bore you with too much of my life's story. But I think you deserve to know a little something about me and how I came to adopt my philosophy on growing and protecting money over six decades on this planet. Only then can I ask you to consider the tips I'll be offering in the following chapters.

It's a cliché to say I came up in the school of hard knocks, but that's my alma mater. That experience made me guarded in the way I approach everything, but especially in dealing with other people's money.

I grew up in San Jose, California, the area I still call home, as the next-to-youngest of seven kids. I had four big brothers, three of whom served in the military during the Vietnam War. I still remember my mother living in daily fear of receiving bad news from the Department of Defense.

We never did have much money. My parents split up before I started high school. By the time my father finally left home, our relationship was pretty strained. I was a big kid, about 6 feet, 3 inches tall in junior high, and he tended to regard me and discipline me as an adult because of that size. I resented it, and he would call me a "hothead" whenever I made my feelings known.

My mom worked hard at a Denny's restaurant to support the family. But she also encountered problems with a man who became interested in her following my father's departure. Her interest didn't match his, however, and when he wouldn't take "no" for an answer, she briefly moved back to her family in Springfield, Mo., to get away from him.

So, at the age of 14, I was largely on my own for two years.

I lived with one of my brothers in a garage apartment. It cost us $25 a month, and we got exactly what we paid for: a small fridge, a two-burner hotplate, a chest of drawers, a bed and a little bathroom. I went to school during the day and managed to play some football and baseball in the afternoon before busting up a knee and ending a decent athletic career. I worked various jobs each night. For a time in high school, I studied at night between doing fill-ups — in a time before self-service — at an ARCO station near the apartment. Later, I joined another guy doing janitorial services at night.

Needless to say, there wasn't time for a typical high school social life. I just couldn't afford to do the screw-up stuff I saw classmates doing, so I didn't tell my friends about my situation. I couldn't exactly tell them, like a lot of kids would have done, "Hey, come over to my place; I'm living without my parents. We'll have a great party." Had the school found out I was living in that kind of situation, I'd have been in foster care very quickly.

My brother and I were able to live like we did for those two years in part because of my size. By high school, I stood about 6 feet, 5 inches, which made people think I was much older than I was. I really wasn't that mature yet; I had a 15-year-old's brain in the body of someone who looked 25. But nobody bothered us during the couple of years when my mom wasn't around.

Still, when Mom wasn't there, we had no one to tell us what to do or not to do. We had to figure things out for ourselves based on a value system we got from our mother. A young man learns to grow up pretty quickly in that kind of situation.

Fighting for the Little Guy

I don't want to suggest that I was always inclined to help people deal with their problems, but I did seem to have a talent for it.

Maybe it started as a bigger little kid. I remember some specific times when I'd see a kid being bullied, and I'd step in to try to break it up. Words didn't always resolve the issue, and there was a time or two I had to whoop someone's butt.

Things became a little more normal when my mother returned to California when I was 16. About five years later, my father — now sober — was back in our lives. But even then, there were problems to be solved after he'd gotten involved in some really bad investments.

Long story short, a guy scammed my folks and my aunt; we spent maybe six years pursuing his case in the courts until he was finally incarcerated.

It was about that time that I started thinking, "If I could help my parents, maybe I could help other people as well." Over time I'd get calls from friends of my parents asking, "Can you help me with this or that?" I was like the painter on the block whose good work is spread through word of mouth. Even before I was licensed to help people look at specific financial products, people were asking me to help them figure out what was going on in their financial lives.

That's also when I began to get wise to what a lot of guys were doing in designing their investment strategies. I didn't like a lot of what I saw.

I didn't get into selling insurance or creating income strategies immediately.

After high school, I began working for the agricultural division of FMC Corporation, which was founded in 1883 by chemist John Bean in Los Gatos, California, as the Bean Spray Pump Company, making piston pumps for insecticides. The company expanded during World War II when it began producing amphibious landing vehicles. In my time at the company's San Jose plant, I worked on both agricultural sprayers and the Bradley Fighting Vehicle that would be used prominently in the First Gulf War and beyond. I was an FMC assembly line foreman around 1989 when I met the man who helped turn my life's road in a new direction. John was selling Medicare supplemental insurance policies when I met him through the Saratoga Sportsman Club, as we had mutual interests in hunting and fishing.

I initially put off his invitations to join him in the insurance business until FMC moved my division out-of-state. Not anxious to relocate from the area in which I'd spent my entire life, I acquired my license to sell insurance and went to work for John. In time, we parted ways and I started my own Platinum Retirement Solutions company in San Jose.

I have never regretted that decision. I've been fortunate enough that my business allows me — and my wife of 30 years, Terri, and our two daughters — to live life on my own terms, both personally and in terms of the way I can help the people I work with build retirement strategies that don't compromise.

Helping people reach their retirement goals is no BS proposition. Simply put, you don't screw around with people's lives or take chances with their money. There is a right way to go about planning for retirement, one that doesn't involve smoke-and-mirrors, and I've worked hard to do things the right way since 1991. That way involves steady and predictable financial products, those without unnecessary exposure to the ups-and-downs of the stock market. Clients need confidence going into retirement, and confidence comes with knowing they have control.

CHAPTER 4

How Much Can You Afford to Lose?

A 55-year-old man walks into a casino ...

(I know, it sounds like the setup to a bad joke. It isn't, so please stay with me.)

He gets lucky early on, winning 100 coins of whatever domination he's playing in one of his first pulls on the slot machine. Now the question becomes, what does he do with that money?

If he's like most players, he figures his luck is running just fine that day, so he keeps pouring that money back into the machine. Over time, he'll win some but likely lose more; remember, the odds always favor the house. If he stays on the floor long enough, he'll likely give back not only the 100 coins of "house money" he won, but probably some of his own gambling stake set aside for that outing.

Now let's look at what might happen had our player applied the investing "Rule of 100" to his gambling approach.

The Rule of 100 is simply stated. You subtract your age from 100, and the remainder is the percentage of investments you can afford to expose to risk — that is, the chance of losing principal — at that stage of your life. Our 55-year-old gambler, using this rule of thumb, should have no more than 45 percent of his retirement portfolio in investments that could lose principal.

There is nothing wrong with being conservative when it comes to your retirement planning.

Applying this rule to our casino example, had this gentleman put 55 of the 100 coins won from his early good fortune immediately into his pocket and kept them there, he could have played with the other 45 coins of "house money" and gone home assured of being at least 55 units ahead of the game.

The point to be made here is that there is nothing wrong with being conservative when it comes to your retirement planning.

That philosophy makes me a different kind of guy from a lot of financial representatives who place their faith — and their clients' money— on the prospect of earning big returns from Wall Street. I'm someone who instead prefers steady, consistent growth. I guess that makes me the tortoise in the storybook race with the hare, but remember who won that race. The story is a fable, obviously, but fables exist to illustrate tenets in life that we might not otherwise see.

Two Steps Forward, Three Steps Back
Is a Dance, Not a Retirement Roadmap

As with our gambler who — in his quest for the big score — gives back his early winnings and eventually parts of his own money, greed can play a devastating role in our financial decisions. I've seen what greed can do to people. I've watched people who thought they knew more than everybody else crash and burn in the dot-com boom and bust, or in the real estate boom that melted down in the sub-prime mortgage mess. Traumatically big losses affect lives.

Imagine if you got on an airplane and the pilot announced, "Ladies and gentlemen, we have a 15 percent chance of crashing this plane before we get to our destination." Would you stay on that plane?

I've said this many times: If you've got a million dollars in your portfolio, and you make another million, it's not going to change who you are. It's not going to dramatically change your spending habits that were created years ago. It's not likely that you'll decide to live lux, become extravagant, and trade in all your old friends for high rollers. But, if you have a million dollars and you lose half a million, that will tremendously affect your lifestyle. Groceries, utilities, eating out, visiting the kids—none of those expenses get cheaper just because your portfolio lost money. Instead, deep cuts to a portfolio must result in cuts to your regular lifestyle spending. That kind of loss is the real deal, and it can happen when people get greedy and want more and more and more.

I once heard someone well versed on investment counseling say that, if you had most of your assets in real estate, you had an 80 to 85 percent chance of surviving even the worst days on Wall Street. Imagine if you got on an airplane and the pilot announced, "Ladies and gentlemen, we have a 15 percent chance of crashing this plane before we get to our destination." Would you stay on that plane?

The same thing applies to your investment dollars. If you want higher returns, you must take on steeper risks. There's an old saying that comes to mind here: pigs get fed; hogs get slaughtered. Unfortunately, people never seem to remember that losses have more impact on your account value than gains. Often, I'll ask people, "If you lose 20 percent of your account value to market dips, how much will it take to get you back to even?" Too many times, they reply "20 percent." But that's not true. If you lose 20 percent of your portfolio, you have less on which to build with the next percent gains, so it will actually take 25 percent to get back to your original starting value.

It's not good enough in retirement planning to take two steps forward if you then take three steps back. Yet, that can happen to people nearing or at retirement age who have too much of their retirement foundation tied to stock market investments that are subject to dramatic fluctuations.

When 2016 opened with the worst January in history — a 1,079-point drop in the Dow Jones Industrial Average was the worst four-day start to a trading year in the history of the index — I don't think it's a stretch to say that many retired people taking income from accounts tied to the market probably weren't sleeping as well each night.[3]

---

[3] Matt Egan, CNN Money. Jan. 7, 2016. "Dow has worst four-day start to a year on record." http://money.cnn.com/2016/01/07/investing/stocks-markets-dow- china/index.html.

As for me, I prefer to keep taking the small steps forward that are provided by insurance-backed products for a portion of assets, examples of which we will discuss in the upcoming chapter. I feel assured knowing my clients with insurance products that protect their principal and provide for steady interest growth likely don't have as much to worry about, financially.

The following chart indicates what it would take to reach even again after a loss, and, as you can see, the steeper the loss, the more extreme the gain needed to recover:

Recovering from a Loss	
If you lose...	You need ___ to regain
10%	11.11%
20%	25%
30%	42.86%
40%	66.67%
50%	100%
60%	150%
70%	233.33%
80%	400%
90%	900%
100%	NOT POSSIBLE

Red Money, Green Money

As the Rule of 100 illustrates, there are times and places in life when you can afford to put more of your money at risk in the hope of earning a better reward.

I often talk to clients in terms of "red money" and "green money." Let's spend a little time talking about each.

Red money is money at risk. By that I mean anything that could lose a dollar. Red money is money we are willing to expose to the market in the hopes of getting a higher return. We accept the possibility of taking losses, even significant ones, if that risk is offset by the chance for greater returns.

Green money is money you can't afford to put at risk. Green money is about protection of your principal. Green money is that for which we are not willing to accept the risk of loss and for which we are willing to accept a lower rate of return. Green money cannot afford to have downside market risks.

Red money is fine for people at younger ages, as that is when we can afford to take more chances in risk/reward investments. When investing on a regular basis in our working years, the theory of dollar-cost averaging says we will buy stocks, bonds, mutual fund shares or exchange-traded funds (ETFs) over different periods when prices are both low and high. Moreover, often market losses during corrections or recessions in our younger years have more time to be potentially offset by market gains over time.

I see far too many people in the pre-retirement phase of life holding too much red money when they should be in green money mode — the conservation phase that precedes the distribution phase.

The key words here are "over time."

People age 55 and older no longer have that kind of time — not in terms of working years — to make up in good market years what they lose in down times. This is the time of life when they need at least a portion of their money to be protected from market downturns yet has some potential to grow.

Yet, I see far too many people in the pre-retirement phase of life holding too much red money when they should be in green money mode — the conservation phase that precedes the distribution phase.

Some don't even know what their exposure to market risk really is. They've got the same investments that performed well for them in their 30s and 40s, and congratulations to them. But now they are moving to a place in life where they need to protect that money, and maybe no one has talked to them about how to do so.

Worse yet, I occasionally see people in their 50s taking some crazy investment risks in the hopes of building up in a short period of time the retirement nest egg they didn't work on years earlier. They are like the gambler at the blackjack table splitting every pair of 10s or doubling down on every opportunity, hoping to win back previous losses.

Transitioning into green money is important in the pre-retirement years, and it is downright essential in retirement. For, this is the time you need to ask yourself: Can I afford to lose any of my retirement fund? If not, you should decide how much, if any, of your money should be in red money.

Granted, not everyone wants all their money in an absolutely guaranteed place. Even in retirement, there are some people willing to expose some money to risk. They still want to "play the game," and are financially comfortable in doing so. Often, the markets are one of the best places to provide a potential hedge against inflation, so having a reasonable portion of your assets in the market may make sense for many.

> *Are you willing to base your future income on speculation or assumptions? Or, would you rather base it on guarantees?*

Yet, I still believe what everyone should have as they approach retirement is a large amount of their retirement money in a solid place where they can never, never lose principal. Moreover, those accounts should strive to provide guarantee a steady rate of return, as well as generate income we can count on for the rest of our lives.

But this can't be guaranteed through the way many folks today save for retirement. That is, by keeping their retirement savings in market-linked IRAs or 401(k)s where they hope to live off an invested pool of money that should, in theory, continue to grow. The bigger hope is that this pool of money will sustain them for the rest of their lives, even as they begin taking distributions from that pool for retirement income.

Now ask yourself this: Are you willing to base your future income on speculation or assumptions? Or, would you rather base it on guarantees?

This is why you often hear retirement professionals say the key to retirement is not in the lump sum you've invested and saved — values that can rise or fall in changing market conditions — but rather in how that money will be used to assure a stream of guaranteed lifetime income you cannot outlive.

One key to doing that is allocating at least a portion of your foundation retirement savings into places where that foundation cannot break down.

That's why we'll talk in the next chapters about different kinds of annuities in which the insurance company writing the annuity contract assumes all the risk of protecting your foundation principal while providing for potential growth. These are contracts with caps, or ceilings, on any interest growth, but also with a floor — of zero — on losses.

We'll also talk about using life insurance not only for its tax-free death benefit to your heirs, but also for the living benefits that you as the policyholder can use for retirement income or long-term care considerations.

We'll talk about taking the guesswork out of creating a retirement income approach, and the sense of comfort and relief that can bring.

CHAPTER 5

From the Mouth of Babe

He will forever be remembered as one of the greatest home run hitters in Major League Baseball history, having belted 714 over 22 seasons. Baseball fans also remember the New York Yankees' "Sultan of Swat" as a pretty good pitcher before his home-run swing and touch-all-bases lifestyle became the biggest parts of his larger-than-life legend.

But how many people know that Babe Ruth also was a pretty shrewd investor?

The Bambino, one of the highest-paid players of his time, is said by insurance industry historians to have purchased his first in a series of annuities with the Equitable Life Insurance Company around 1923. Reports from that era say he often invested up to half of his annual salary, amounts between $35,000 and $50,000 a year, until 1929.[4]

You know what happened in 1929. The stock market crash in late October of that year jump-started the Great Depression, and millions of people saw much of their life savings wiped out by the collapse of banks and other financial institutions.

---

[4] Center for Annuity Awareness. "Babe Ruth Homers with Annuities." https://www.annuityawareness.com/benefits-annuities/babe-ruth-homers-annuities.

Ruth, however, was a financial survivor of that carnage, as were the insurance companies who guaranteed the money he had invested as well as the promise to provide him income for the rest of his life. Ruth and his wife, Clara, are said to have lived a comfortable lifestyle long after his 1935 retirement, largely in part because of the monthly annuity payments he received from the insurance company.

"I take many risks in life," the Babe was quoted as saying, "but I never risk my money."

Inside the Promise of Annuities

Having made my case in previous chapters about the need to protect a portion of your retirement savings and assure a flow of guaranteed lifetime income from those assets, let me state what I believe to be one reasonable way to accomplish both goals.

There is no investment on the planet that can do what an annuity can do in terms of guaranteed income. Let me say upfront, however, that annuities are not right for everyone. While I believe they offer significant benefits to a retirement portfolio, they need to be carefully evaluated against your needs, objectives, tax situation, and many more factors before deciding if an annuity makes sense for you.

So, let's examine how they work:

There are basically four places to put your money: banks, real estate, insurance companies and Wall Street. Banks are considered "safe," but they also pay little interest on certificates of deposits in the low-interest world that followed the Great Recession of 2008. Real estate isn't something you typically put in an IRA. We've just talked at length about how Wall Street offers no guarantees, even though one can do well there in good market years. Still, as you cruise into retirement and your earning power becomes limited when you're not working anymore, you no longer have time to recover the losses incurred during inevitable market downturns.

So, what do you do with your market-exposed IRA or 401(k) monies if you want conservative growth opportunity and a guaranteed source of income for you and your spouse for the rest of your lives?

You might just do what the Babe did. You go to an insurance company.

You purchase an annuity contract in which you agree to give the insurance company a sum of money, which is called the premium. The company in turn agrees to protect that money from any downside risk — except in the case of variable annuities, which we discuss later in this chapter — and agrees to pay tax-deferred interest or interest tied to the movement of an external market index on that premium for as long as you hold the annuity. When you begin to take income from an annuity funded by post-tax dollars, you pay tax only on the interest earned, not the premium invested. When you take income from an annuity funded with pre-tax dollars, all funds withdrawn will be subject to ordinary income taxes. Note also that any withdrawals will be subject to a surrender in the earlier years of the contract and could also incur a 10 percent tax penalty for withdrawals before your age 59 1/2.

How can an insurance company make and keep that kind of promise?

Solvency by definition means a company has enough funds or liquid assets with which to pay all of its debts.

The backbone of any annuity is the claims-paying reliability of an insurance company, most of which have withstood the test of time despite world wars, natural disasters, depressions/recessions and the collapse of other financial institutions. This can be attributed in no small part to the legal cash reserves they must keep on hand to maintain solvency, as well as the regulations and oversight under which they operate in each of the 50 states.

The financial stability of insurance companies — something you need to consider before deciding to purchase an annuity contract from that company — can be assessed in several ways.

One is the rating given to each company as determined by independent rating agencies such as A.M. Best, Standard and Poor, Moody's, and Fitch. I have some personal concerns about these ratings, as they are solicited by the insurance companies. That means a company can ask to be rated by one of the agencies, giving it the opportunity to put its books in good order before the rating agency makes its inspection.

I recommend that consumers looking to evaluate the strength of an insurance company look instead at the solvency rating of each company. Solvency by definition means a company has enough funds or liquid assets with which to pay all of its debts. For insurance companies, a positive solvency rating means it has more in legal reserves than it has in obligations to pay on its claims or annuity contracts.

Solvency ratings are determined by the insurance department of each state in which an insurance company does business. State inspectors can march unannounced into a company every three years and demand a look at the company's books. I like the idea that an insurance company doesn't know the state inspectors are coming.

This regulatory function addresses one of the problems I have with Wall Street, where, in my opinion, there isn't nearly enough oversight on what some of these money managers are doing. The Securities and Exchange Commission is supposed to be a kind of policeman, but what are they policing? When you see people on Wall Street arrested for Ponzi schemes, you wonder how the SEC or the industry itself opened the door to let people function that way.

Who was watching Bernie Madoff? How could no one have been paying attention to what he was doing? Obviously, it's not possible to uncover every possible instance of potential financial crime or negligence, but I'm still surprised by how long some of these companies were able to continue to do business before they were caught.

An Effective but Tricky Tool to Use

Annuities are excellent tools for retirement income, but they can be complicated and difficult to understand for many people.

This is especially true when it comes time to start taking income from an annuity. There are many common annuitization options in which to take income — life, life with period certain, life with survivor benefits, and period-certain, just to mention a few. They all have different effects on how you take income, which can be for life, if you set it up accordingly. We will talk in greater detail about the different ways of taking income in our Chapter 8 discussion on distributions.

What too many people don't understand is that, once you begin taking withdrawals from some older annuities — generally ones purchased before 2008 when the "income rider" option became available — the annuity contract morphs into a different kind of process. This happens when you convert the asset to income in a process called annuitizing. The guaranteed growth you experienced prior to making withdrawals changes. Moreover, you lose control over the asset, as the insurance company now controls its distribution.

Understanding when and how to best exercise your distribution options becomes even more difficult when the person who sold you the annuity is no longer available — through retirement, relocation or just getting out of the business — to explain those options. Suddenly, the annuitant may not have someone he can count on to help him. He can call the insurance company and have someone explain the different distribution options, but he has no one with whom to discuss which options are truly best for him.

Without an income strategy in place, an annuitant may not fully understand how best to take his distributions. With an income strategy in place, however, an annuitant should expect to fully understand exactly how his income flow will be handled, even if he no longer has access to the insurance agent who sold him the annuity.

This is why I believe it's important for anyone holding an annuity contract or planning to purchase one to get with an agent who works mainly in the annuity arena and truly understands the new vehicles that are available. That is especially the case with the fixed indexed annuity that features income riders — options that guarantee the growth of the amount from which you will eventually be able to withdraw income, and which allow you to begin taking income without annuitizing the contract. (We will discuss the role of income riders in the next section.)

Keep in mind that, in many annuities purchased before 2008 or thereabouts, the income riders available now were not available then. Some people with older annuities may want to consider if it makes sense for their situation to transfer their money through a 1035 exchange or direct transfer from an older annuity to a newer indexed annuity that has growth and distribution options not available previously. Some of these options include the guaranteed roll-up we will talk about that increases the contract's income withdrawal amount.

Is it smart for everyone to switch out of long-held annuities? Not necessarily. But it is smart to examine your options to see if this could be good for you. Knowledge is power, and you need to know about options with newer annuities that can work to your advantage. If you have an annuity purchased, say, 10 years ago that is paying 3 percent, and you plan to use this annuity for income in future years, if you have the chance to transfer it to one that would roll up your income value by 7 percent without paying a substantial penalty on the original annuity, it just makes sense to do it. On the other hand, there are older fixed annuities in which the fixed interest rate could be better than anything offered in a newer fixed annuity issued in the era of low interest rates that followed the Great Recession.

Additional variables are worthy of consideration.

It's possible to be "handcuffed" to a contract you own by the surrender charges that come when leaving an old contract for a newer one. Let's explain that.

All annuities come with surrender charges that can be as high as 8 to 10 percent or more for surrendering the contract in the first year. That surrender penalty generally decreases over time until there is no surrender charge after a number of years, which can vary from four to 10 years or more depending on the insurance company. If you are out of the surrender phase, it may make sense to make a transfer. But if you are looking at a heavy surrender charge to transfer from one annuity to another, a transfer may not make sense.

Again, each individual situation can vary. That's why it is important to do your research and find out if the transfer is something that works well for you. But you won't know until you talk to someone with expertise in the annuity arena.

The point is, you need to consider all your options and choose those that will improve your retirement income. Again, you need to talk to someone well acquainted with the complex field of annuities to help you understand your best options.

Different Products for Different Needs

There are many different kinds of annuities to serve different needs. The trick is picking one that works well for your specific need at different times of your life.

The Fixed Annuity

A fixed annuity — which Babe Ruth generally employed — pays a fixed interest rate, generally around 3 percent in recent years. They've been higher during periods of higher interest trends.

The Immediate Annuity

With an immediate annuity, you give an insurance company a sum of money —and the insurance company begins paying you income immediately (within the first year, generally) for a pre-determined period of time. You can determine that time frame — life, or life with period certain, or whatever option you chose.

They key here is to understand that an immediate annuity is immediately annuitized, meaning no changes can be made to your distribution option once you make it. There is no going back. You can't take cash out of the account, only annuitized income.

These annuities are less common, but they are available for people who want to convert a pool of money into a promise of income guaranteed over a period of time. That time period can be for the rest of your life, with the understanding that when you die all income payments stop. The time period can be "life with period certain," meaning that if the period is 10 years and you die before that period ends, money continues to be paid to a beneficiary for up to 10 years. If you live beyond the 10 years (or 20, or however long you select), the income continues to be paid until the time of your death.

The Variable Annuity

A variable annuity is more aggressive and offers the prospect of higher returns through exposure to the stock market. Remember, though, with market exposure comes the risk of loss, which means variable annuities could lose their original value. Variable annuities are often viewed as having a higher fee structure and you will pay those fees whether the annuity performs well or not.

But variable annuities have changed over the years.

Many newer variable annuities — those issued since about 2008 and after — feature income rider options that make them more attractive to some people. But this option is not cheap. A variable annuity income rider that guarantees a 5 percent roll up for income can cost 1 percent to 1.25 percent just to own it. Add that rider fee to the policy fee, mutual fund fees and sub-account fees — just to mention a few of the various possible fees — and it's common to see variable annuities today with total fees of up to 4 percent a year.

The bigger problem is, most people with a variable annuity don't understand this fee structure until they get together with someone doing the due diligence necessary to detail all those fees.

Still, variable annuities have their place for some. But, they also can lose money, especially with older contracts that do not have income riders. Variable annuities are what they are, and if they work in your situation, by all means, consider them.

But even with the high fee structure, there can be some compelling reasons to hang onto a variable annuity you've had for some time. That's especially true when considering the annuity's death benefit, which can be of great value to the annuity holder.

I had a client holding a variable annuity whose husband was in a nursing home with Alzheimer's disease. The cash value in her account had fallen to maybe $90,000, but it carried a death benefit on her husband of $190,000, which was the highest value of the account in all the years she owned it.

That death benefit is always something to consider when you talk about moving out of a variable annuity. Your cash value may decline in bad-market times, but the death benefit remains at a level such that you may want to consider keeping it.

The Indexed Annuity

Indexed annuities, also known as fixed index typically offer better interest potential than fixed-rate annuities. They also offer a death benefit and protection against loss of principal. Their prospect for greater interest potential is due to their interest being calculated based on an external stock market index such as the S&P 500, the Dow Jones Industrial Average, the Russell 2000, the NASDAQ or any number of others.

In a good market year, your account is credited with interest that is tied to a percentage of the index growth. Because the insurance company assumes the risk against loss of your principal, fixed indexed annuities place a limit on the amount of interest you will earn – usually in the form of a cap (also known as a ceiling), spread or participation rate. For example: If the index strategy in your annuity increases by 9 percent over the contract year, your interest credit may be capped at, say, 6 percent. But, you also have a protection against loss — your floor — which is no loss at all.

Consider what that meant to the holder of a fixed indexed annuity in the market collapse of 2007-08. He experienced capped interest potential in the years leading up to the bursting of the sub-prime mortgage bubble but lost nothing in the annuity when the market experienced dramatic losses (provided he didn't surrender the contract or take excessive withdrawals). He didn't make anything in the worst of times, but neither did he lose. Zero is your hero, in this case.

Other indexed strategies offer interest potential through an option called the "spread." This strategy says, if you choose this option, it will pay you as much in interest as that index makes in a year with a spread of, say, 2.25 percent. That means the first 2.25 percent goes to the insurance company, and you get the rest regardless of how high the index rises. Note that if the index returns 2.25% or less, in this situation, you will earn zero for the year.

It is important to understand the intricacies of caps, participation rates and spreads in an individual annuity contract before entering into one.

Some policies give the annuitant an option on which crediting method (or strategy) to use, and most people need an insurance professional well-versed on the complexities of annuities to explain the difference.

Here, in short, is how it works.

Insurance companies calculate the growth in a market index in any number of ways, most involving a point-to-point accounting.

One such method is done annually, in the annuity anniversary. The S&P 500, for example, was at point A on Jan. 30, 2015, and at point B on Jan. 29, 2016. If the index grows from point A to point B by, say, 7 percent, your account is credited with interest capped at, say, 4 percent (or whatever the contract designates). If the index gain is only 2 percent, you get that much interest. Conversely, you lose nothing if the index shows a negative return in that 12-month period. (Keep in mind, though, that if you elect an income rider for your annuity, the fee for that rider will come out of your annuity value every year, even in year's where there is no interest credited).

An alternative crediting method uses a monthly point-to-point accounting system.

In this method, the change in the S&P 500 — our example index — is calculated from Jan. 15 to Feb. 14, then again from Feb. 15 to March 14 and so on throughout the year. The monthly interest is capped Say, with a monthly cap of 1.5%, and the monthly gain in an index is 3 percent. Your interest opportunity for that month is capped at 1.5 percent. It's the most you can make in a given month. But in a real boom year, these monthly amounts can add up.

There is always a downside. In this case, let's say you experienced 1.5 percent interest in each of the years' first four months. You're looking at a nice potential 6 percent interest credit. But come May, the market sees a significant downturn and loses 6 percent. You're now back at zero.

The following chart shows us the power of that "zero is your hero" concept, demonstrating a $100,000 fixed index annuity with an annual cap of 8 percent against the performance of a $100,000 investment in products that follow the S&P 500 directly and are subject to market loss. This example doesn't include any fees and reflects a guaranteed minimum of $100,000.

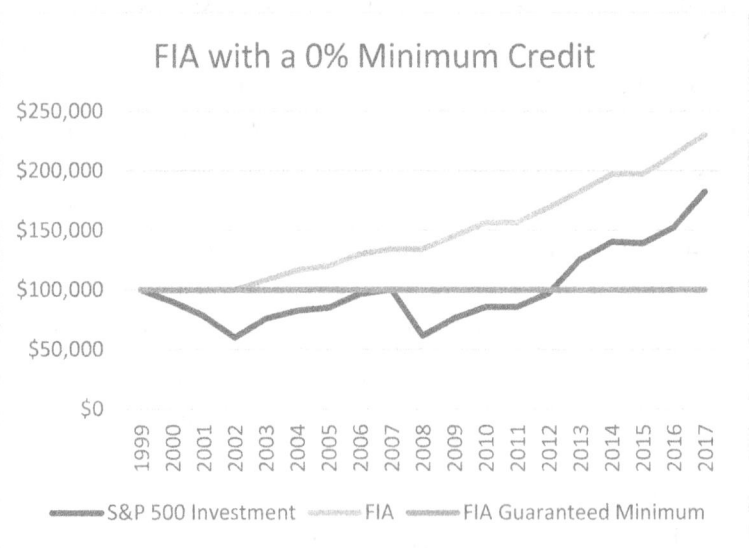

Keep in mind, though, that with the option of an income rider (for an additional annual cost), your income value is guaranteed to grow each year for the purpose of taking income by a specified percentage, regardless of what the market index does. But you could also see additional growth to the annuity's base cash value beyond the guaranteed roll up in times of a strong, performing market.

Remember, this is all about how you choose to leverage your money, to do what makes sense for you without the risk of losing principal.

The Coming of the Income Rider

I promised earlier to explain "income riders" in more detail. Let's do that now.

Fixed indexed annuities provide the chance to consider an optional benefit known as the "income rider." These options can be complicated but, in short, they are an added-on option — one that comes with a fee of up to generally around 1-2 percent — that says the insurance company will provide you a lifetime income stream that you can begin to tap at some point in the future.

A lot of people, in my opinion, don't understand...and consequently use this tool for the wrong purpose.

Insurance companies created these income riders several years ago. They are based on the concept of a "roll up," a guaranteed rate of annual interest growth in income value that compounds during the accumulation years of the annuity. The roll up rates usually are guaranteed only until you reach a certain age or when you begin to take withdrawals.

It is important here to understand how these fixed indexed contracts grow in terms of cash and credits. Many people don't fully comprehend the difference.

Consider it this way. Draw a line down the middle of a piece of paper. On the left side put the word "cash." This represents the cash value of your annuity and is determined by the interest you earn due to your selected index option. In a down market year, you may see no interest, but you will also see no loss other than the rider fee that is deducted from the cash accumulation side of the annuity.

Now, on the other side of the vertical line write the word "income" and a figure of, let's say, 7 percent. What this means is that, as long as you're not taking income from the annuity, the income value of the contract — also known as the "benefit side" or "income accumulation value" — will experience compounded interest growth each year of around 7 percent (or whatever the roll-up figure available in your contract) until you begin taking withdrawals.

Bear in mind that the left side of the contract represents hard money, your actual cash in the annuity, should you choose to surrender your contract (and before any surrender charges are applied). The right side represents interest credits to your income value, a level of compounded interest growth you'll see in income value regardless of what happens to the cash value side.

This distinction is important because if you die and pass on the money in the annuity to a non-spousal heir, they will receive only the cash value. The right (income value) side is not "real money" to take as a lump sum but represents the value from which the annuity holder can take future income.

A lot of people, in my opinion, don't understand the difference and consequently use this tool for the wrong purpose. They hear about 7 percent growth and think in terms of cash they can take out of the annuity in 10 years or so. That's not how it works. The cash value figure isn't assured of growing 7 percent every year. Only the right-hand income side has the guaranteed roll up that comes into play for the purpose of taking income.

What Does This Mean to You?

Let's look at some hypothetical case studies.

Let's say a client first came to me at age 62 with around $450,000 in his IRA account. He was worried, as he should have been, that if he withdrew the recommended 4 percent each year from an account that didn't have guarantees to his principal, he might run out of money if he lived as long as life expectancy tables think he will.

After discussing his future income needs and the benefits of an annuity, he decided to use a portion of this money to purchase a fixed index annuity. He also purchased an optional income rider which offered a 7 percent roll ups to the income value each year. Using the Rule of 72 — a financial rule of thumb that says you can determine approximately how long it will take a figure to double by dividing 72 by the figure's rate of return — this gentleman's $450,000 annuity income value could double in a little more than 10 years (72 divided by 7). (Remember, this is the value that he can use to draw income. The 7 percent roll-up applies to the value for income purposes and is not available if decides to surrender the annuity for cash).

Let's look at another case. Let's assume we have a gentleman who is age 56 and his goal was to have $100,000 a year in income by the time he retired at age 66, his full retirement age for Social Security purposes. How, he asked, can he get there?

We discussed various financial options and strategies, including the use of a fixed index annuity (FIA). He agreed that an FIA with an income rider was the right approach for him.

At age 56, he decided to purchase this type of annuity with $500,000 from transferring funds out of a side investment. With a

7 percent yearly roll up to the income rider value, the rule of 72 suggests his income value should double to $1 million in 10 years, his target date for retirement. A withdrawal rate of 5.4 percent on $1 million is $56,831 a year for life, a rate provided by the income rider even if the annuity itself doesn't earn any indexed interest. Add that to his Social Security income and other investment dividends, the man was well on his way to his retirement income target.

Don't Believe Everything You Hear

Look, if people want to tell you annuities are bad because of fees or complexities or whatever concerns they have, I can't stop them. But let's be honest about other aspects of the investment world. Stocks and bonds can be bad. Mutual funds can be bad. Everything is bad when times are bad, just as everything's swell when times are good.

What it ultimately boils down to is this: What are you trying to accomplish, and do you have the right vehicle to get you there?

Again, when we're being task-oriented, and you tell me where you want to be 10 years from now, it's my job to give you suggestions about how to get there. You may not like what I'm telling you, but facts are facts.

That's why I say you must build your foundation of retirement income on fact, not speculation.

I believe, when it's possible to create cash flow and income for life with a portion of your assets without having to worry about Wall Street's hurdles, it's worth considering.

Now, I'm not suggesting that everyone reading this book take all their money and rush it into fixed indexed annuities. But I am saying they have a definite place in the plans of many people nearing or in retirement. Anyone who hopes to retire successfully eventually has to come to terms with where their money is and how it's doing. More importantly, we need to know what it will do in the future. Annuities can help remove some of that uncertainty.

I've just seen too many people come into my office for a first consultation and show me their IRA or 401(k) statements where all their assets are in stocks, bonds or mutual funds, none of which carry any guarantees of future returns.

Most of those holdings are based on an advisor at XYZ Financial telling you what he thinks is best for you. But really, it's not his sole responsibility to see that your account performs — it's yours. The liability is ultimately on your shoulders, not his. He can't be sued if the market goes down. You can't spank him when things go wrong.

Knowing all we know about stock market volatility, we should understand that placing our money with Wall Street is based strictly on hope. We're hoping that the market performs to the point that we have enough to retire, ideally based on carefully calculated risks. But you can't afford to base your entire retirement plans solely on hope. You need to rely on facts, and the facts are that the market will go up and it will go down and, as that happens, you will pay a guy X amount of dollars in fees whether your brokerage account goes up or down.

To be sure, there are people who enjoy the stock market challenge, the running and jumping over obstacles like a high hurdler in track. There are others who prefer to circle the track without all that jumping.

I believe that, when it's possible to create cash flow and income for life with a portion of your assets without having to worry about Wall Street's hurdles, it's worth considering.

CHAPTER 6

Take a New Look at Life Insurance

ome of you reading this may not remember the days of the door-to-door salesman. Consider yourself fortunate if you don't.

Recalling that era requires going back in time 50 years or more. Salesmen would knock uninvited at your house, peddling everything from vacuum cleaners to household cleaning products. Many people never let them in the door.

Another thing often sold door-to-door in those days was life insurance. That explains in part why life insurance got a bad name with many people who remember — and likely resent — the pesky salesmen who interrupted family dinners or evenings in front of the TV.

Detracting further from the reputation of life insurance is the fact that the term insurance or whole life insurance policies offered by the salesmen of that era weren't necessarily the greatest product for everyone due to their lack of flexibility. People bought them to provide financial protection for their families, knowing those policies would be often of little value until the insured person was dead.

Some whole and universal life insurance policies were sold on the prospect that the cash growth in a policy over the years — the result of investment growth experienced by the insurance company — would eventually allow the insured to stop paying premiums, a nice selling point. Until, that is, the policies didn't experience enough cash growth to pay the premiums. The insured person would then get notices from the insurance company asking for premium payments to keep a policy from lapsing, causing many people to eventually cancel the policy.

It's not surprising, then, to hear people of a certain age say today, "Why would I want to consider life insurance at my advanced age?"

Well, times have changed, and life insurance has changed. Today, many life insurance policies have what are called "living benefits" that offer value to an insured person while they are alive, as well as providing the traditional financial protection to your family when you die.

The living benefits of today's life insurance policies can be used to help people in many ways that were unavailable at the time our parents were turning away salesmen at the door. I would go as far as to say that people who haven't taken a fresh look at the living benefits of today's life insurance policies are missing the boat by failing to see favorable aspects that are now available in the financial services industry.

Let's look at some important ways life insurance can be a useful tool in building a retirement strategy.

Life Insurance as an Income Source

Life insurance will always be first and foremost a product that provides a death benefit for loved ones. Unlike many other financial products, it involves fees and charges in exchange for offering a death benefit. But today's policies offer other benefits, as well.

Today we have policies known as "indexed universal life insurance" (IUL) that have the ability to earn interest tied to the movement of an external market index, similar to how an FIA earns interest. This gives you the potential greater interest over a period of time than might a whole-life policy with a fixed interest rate of, say, 3 percent with dividend reinvestment. In good market years, the IUL's upside potential for cash value growth — that is, the growth of the money you pay into that policy as premiums — can be quite competitive. The growing cash value of these IUL policies can be used to accomplish a couple of things.

The policy still pays a death benefit — tax-free money — to the insured's survivors. But it also provides the opportunity to do some helpful things while the insured is still alive, one of which is to provide an additional source of income that can be beneficial at retirement.

Unlike many other financial products, [life insurance] involves fees and charges in exchange for offering a death benefit. But today's policies offer other benefits, as well.

Indexed universal life policies — which unlike 401(k)s, IRAs or Roth IRAs have no limit on how much you "invest" in the form of premiums — have something called policy loan provisions. These provisions allow the policy owner to take tax-free loans from a portion of the policy's cash value as a source of supplemental retirement income. At the time of the insured's death, the policy's death benefit is used first to repay any policy loans — money used while the insured was alive. The remaining balance of the death benefit is then paid tax-free to the beneficiaries of the insured.

It is important to note here that such loans reduce the policy's accumulated cash value, as well as affect the death benefit and could cause the policy to lapse or require additional premiums. An insured person considering taking such loans has to decide, in effect, whether he wants to use some of that insurance while he is alive, or leave all of it for his beneficiaries after his death.

Among the advantages of using the living benefits while still alive:

- A source of tax-free income.
- Tax-deferred growth of the cash value, which continues even after you begin taking loans or withdrawals. No IRS contribution limits; no required distributions after age 70½; no premature distribution penalties before age 59.
- Protection from market loss.
- Finally, the traditional insurance protection of tax-free income for the insured's beneficiaries.

Let's consider one example of how an indexed universal life policy might work.

Let's look at a 48-year old woman and her husband, who had a combined annual income of just over $200,000. They were interested in the death benefit that life insurance provides for their estate planning needs, as well as generating tax-free income in retirement. They made too much in annual income to be able to make contributions to a Roth IRA — a common source of tax-free money. They could have gravitated toward municipal bonds, but in the low-interest climate after the Great Recession, those bonds weren't returning much money.

As an alternative, she and I talked about purchasing a fixed index universal life insurance policy with a $6,000 annual premium. Her plan is, after 18 years, at her full retirement age (66) she can take tax free income from the policy as a supplement to her other retirement income. (This assumes no prior withdrawals are made, the policy remains in force, and it has performed well during this time.) In addition, at her death, the remaining death benefit is available to help support her legacy and estate planning goals.[5]

Life Insurance as a Supplement to Social Security

It's not uncommon for me to meet with people who worry that some government entitlement programs — namely Social Security and Medicare — may not be there for them in their present form when they're at full retirement age. (To calculate your own full retirement age, take a look at the chart on the following page.)

Let's look at yet another situation.

I prepared a plan for a man who wanted to put $500 a year into an IUL for his daughter at age 15. At age 25, she would take over payments when she has her own career. He is allowed to transfer the contract to her; it becomes her asset, her responsibility. If she maintains the investment, she will have an additional source of income if she needs it, which she likely will if safety net entitlement programs aren't there for members of her generation at retirement age.

Let me go on record here to suggest I believe that members of her generation, as well as people in their 30s and 40s should to start looking at how they can provide guaranteed retirement income for

---

[5] Policy loans and withdrawals will reduce available cash values and death benefits, and may cause the policy to lapse or affect any guarantees against lapse. Additional premium payments may be required to keep the policy in force. In the event of a lapse, outstanding policy loans in excess of unrecovered cost basis will be subject to ordinary income tax. Tax laws are subject to change. You should consult a tax professional.

themselves if Social Security provides less for them — or if it starts at a later time in life — than it did for their parents.

To calculate your own full retirement age, you can check the following chart:[6]

Your Full Retirement Age	
Year of Birth	**Full Retirement Age**
1937 or earlier	65
1938	65 and 2 months
1939	65 and 4 months
1940	65 and 6 months
1941	65 and 8 months
1942	65 and 10 months
1943—1954	66
1955	66 and 2 months
1956	66 and 4 months
1957	66 and 6 months
1958	66 and 8 months
1959	66 and 10 months
1960 or later	67

Don't misunderstand. I don't believe Social Security will be completely eliminated. But, I do believe it will change. When you think back to our parents and grandparents, many often first claimed Social Security at age 62 back in a day when life expectancy was around 67. Then the government pushed the benefits age back to 64, then 65, 66 and it's going up even more for younger people. Will we eventually see the age for maximum benefits pushed back beyond 70? We don't know.

What we do know is there are projections that the Social Security coffers will be broke by 2033. That means benefits will be

---

[6] Social Security Administration. 2018. "Full Retirement Age." https://www.ssa.gov/planners/retire/retirechart.html.

reduced by as much as 20-25 percent, unless changes are made before then. Where will the money to pay the full Social Security benefits come from then? Consider, too, the other retirement-related changes we've seen. The defined-benefit pension system all but went away (for most people) and was replaced by the 401(k) that said, in effect, now you have to work on and fund the majority of your own retirement. Beyond that, you're also now exposed to the whims of the stock market, which is good at times and not so good at others.

So now it's up to the consumer to look after himself. That means, if you don't have enough sense to look ahead, to make sure you're where you need to be on the road to retirement, shame on you.

If you're planning your future entirely around Wall Street, well, that's not what I would do, personally. But if you're 31, say, and worried Social Security may not be there for you in retirement 30 years from now, you need to consider some alternative financial products to help you get to where you need to be.

You might consider talking to someone like me to address the issue, for in that conversation we might well talk about the advantages of the IUL. You get death benefit protection for your family, tax-free future income later in your life, and you're also getting possible long-term care protection.

Which brings us to the next advantage of today's life insurance policies.

Life Insurance to Supplement Long-Term Care Needs

In today's world, where medical and health care advances have increased our life expectancy, the prospect of someday needing long-term health care — whether for yourself or a spouse — is one of the most pressing concerns of people near or in retirement. The rapidly rising costs of long-term care, whether in a skilled nursing facility or via in-home care, is a financial obligation that can quickly drain a pool of retirement money.

Long-term-care insurance policies were the traditional first hedge against the potentially budget-busting costs of nursing home care. Their premiums were never cheap, and they've tended to increase as more and more aging baby boomers demand them.

In some cases, those premiums have since grown to the point that I've had clients who can no longer pay the premiums on long-term care policies they've held for 15 years. These are people who had the foresight to buy the policy during their working years when they paid, say, $1,200 a year in premiums. By 2015, however, that premium may be $4,500 a year, a price they can no longer afford in retirement.

Moreover, long-term-care policies are a use-it-or-lose-it proposition. If you don't eventually need long-term care, the money you spent is essentially "wasted." You don't get a refund. If you can no longer afford the premiums, the policy lapses and, again, the money you spent is gone. This is why I see many clients looking for alternatives to these policies.

IUL can be just such an alternative.

The living benefits of some IULs feature either "accelerated benefits" or a long-term-care rider — options usually requiring an additional fee. Note we have to say "some IULs" because these riders are not available in all states or on all IULs in states that allow such riders.

In short, IULs with long-term-care (LTC) riders allow a portion of the death benefit — typically 2 percent per month — to be used to defray long-term care expenses. Policies with accelerated benefits may allow the insured to double that amount, to use up to 4 percent of his death benefit each month to help pay LTC needs.

Let's look at an example of how it might work.

Let's say you're now paying $3,000 a year for an individual, traditional LTC policy, and you know that premium will only rise in upcoming years. Let's examine what happens if you instead put that $3,000 annually into an IUL that has a $300,000 death benefit.

Now what do you have? First, you know that if you die prematurely, a $300,000 tax-free benefit is paid to your survivors. You also know that if you become ill or impaired to the point that you need nursing care, you can typically extract 2 percent each month $6,000 from a $300,000 death benefit — to defray some of your nursing costs. If your policy has accelerated benefits, that monthly number can double.

At some point down the road, if your need for long-term care is extensive, that $300,000 death benefit could run out. When that happens, the death benefit coverage for your beneficiaries is gone. But, you at least were able to use your insurance coverage when you needed it most, at a time of life when the financial burden of nursing care could be overwhelming.

Note, too, there are some annuity products that also offer provisions for long-term health care. Some also offer doubled accelerated benefits for long-term care.

Here's another way to consider it. If your annual income from a $750,000 annuity is $30,000, and you need nursing care or home care, wouldn't it be nice to have that $30,000 in income turn into $60,000 for nursing care expenses? Many newer annuities have this feature.

Cast Off the Old Stereotypes

The bottom line is that life insurance policies today are more often viable, and thus more attractive, because of their living benefits provisions. They can really make a difference as part of a retirement approach, both in providing a source of tax-free income and for helping to pay for long-term health care, in addition to the traditional death benefit feature.

Is life insurance the definitive solution to long-term health care? No, it is not. But it can take some of the sting out of the expense based upon the amount of death benefit you are able to purchase.

The key is, if you're going to buy life insurance as one component of a retirement plan, make sure you buy the right kind of policy, one with the potential to grow your cash value and provide living benefits.

Remember, not every product is good for everybody. John Doe may want long-term-care insurance, but he doesn't have enough money to put into a vehicle like an annuity, or he can't afford to purchase a life insurance policy because the annual premium is too high at his age. So, perhaps a long-term-care policy is more advantageous to him. (Note that both the life insurance and the LTC insurance may require him to qualify for the coverage medically, so in most cases he will need to be healthy enough for this.)

Conversely, a guy with a 401(k) account of, say, a half-million dollars set aside for long term care expenses might put that money into an annuity. He plans to start taking income in five years when that income account value has grown to $700,000. He can do so knowing that the roughly $30,000 he'll take in annual income (hypothetically) will double to $60,000 for long-term care if he needs it. He is a very viable candidate for this annuity kind of option, assuming it's suitable for him otherwise

Another guy might be able to afford the $6,000 to $7,000 a year in premiums on a life insurance policy that carries a $250,000 (hypothetical) death benefit. He pays his premiums knowing he can extract 2 percent of that $250,000 every month for long-term care until that death benefit is exhausted.

Never Too Late to Start

All of these things we've just been talking about — whether solving for retirement income or for long-term care — are part of a task we're trying to accomplish.

Many times a client will ask, "Aren't I too old now to be considering life insurance?" No question, it's often better to begin sooner than later, yet it's never too late to get something started. How you do it depends on the task you're working on. Let's say you're 55 and trying to produce generate tax-free income in retirement. If you're single and making more than $80,000 a year, or $160,000 as a couple, you can't make contributions to a Roth IRA. The opportunity to secure a death benefit as well as make unlimited contributions and higher premium payments to an IUL might be attractive to you — even at this time of life — knowing you have the potential to generate a tax-free income stream from policy loans in later years.

Now let's consider another hypothetical couple at age 55, with this pair wondering if they have enough money for retirement.

They've gone through the typical phases of life. In their 20s they started a family, spent their 30s paying for typical family needs, then struggled to provide college funds in their 40s. Now as they approach retirement in their 50s, they start to wonder how they can afford to live the rest of their lives after the paychecks stop coming in another 10 years or so.

These are folks who might typically balk at paying insurance premiums at this point in their lives. And yet, there is nothing to keep people 55, 60 or even older from buying life insurance as a way of leveraging the dollars spent on premiums to help grow that money and eventually potentially provide another source of retirement income, or as a means to defray health care expenses, in addition to providing a death benefit for estate planning needs.

There is one other use of the insurance option to consider in retirement.[7]

It involves the money the IRS says we must begin taking in required minimum distributions (RMDs) from tax-qualified accounts beginning at age 70½. We'll look in more detail at the tax implications of RMDs in the next chapter, but for now consider the situation of an individual or couple that doesn't have an immediate need for the taxable money they are required to take from IRAs or 401(k)s. What are they to do with it?

Here is a situation where that person(s) might consider reinvesting that RMD money into a properly structured life insurance policy such as an IUL. The RMD money once again grows tax free and will never again be taxed when taken as a distribution, assuming the policy qualifies as life insurance and is not considered a modified endowment contract. The policy provides a death benefit for heirs, offers the potential for a tax-free income stream if needed, and offers some assistance to defray long-term nursing costs.

The living benefits of today's life insurance policies offer many attractive options for people in or near retirement. And yet many people still think of life insurance the way they did when they were younger, when policies offered little for the insured during his lifetime. In today's environment, however, the premiums paid on life insurance products such as the IUL should be considered as an opportunity to enjoy additional benefits during your lifetime.

---

[7] Policy loans and withdrawals will reduce available cash values and death benefits, and may cause the policy to lapse or affect any guarantees against lapse. Additional premium payments may be required to keep the policy in force. In the event of a lapse, outstanding policy loans in excess of unrecovered cost basis will be subject to ordinary income tax. Tax laws are subject to change. You should consult a tax professional.

CHAPTER 7

Pay Me Now or Pay Me Later: Taxes in Retirement

I spend a good deal of time in my seminars and presentations talking about Roth IRA conversions.

I talk to people who have a good understanding of why these conversions are a good idea, and I talk to people who are hearing about the concept for the first time. After all the talking is done, I find a lot of common ground among the people who know a lot, those who know a little, and those who know very little at all.

The common ground is, few of them want to pay taxes now in order to do an IRA conversion that can work to their advantage later. It's part of why Roth conversions scare some people.

Let's briefly first define the concept of the Roth IRA and the Roth conversion.

For the majority of people with the foresight to invest in their retirement during their working years, the bulk of the money they've invested through an IRA, a 401(k) or 403(b) has been tax-deferred money. Each pay period, people participating in these programs have money deducted before the government taxes it — a nice tax break during your accumulation years.

The common ground is, few [near retirement] want to pay taxes now in order to do an IRA conversion that can work to their advantage later.

That money, along with any matching amount your employer may contribute in a 401(k), grows tax-deferred in whatever investment vehicles you or your company's plan chooses, be it market-based or fixed income or some combination. That money is not taxed until you begin taking distributions or withdrawals from the account. These distributions will happen most frequently in retirement at a time when — in theory, anyway — your tax rate should be lower than when you were working.

You can begin taking this money any time, though there are significant penalties for doing so (in most cases) if you make withdrawals before age 59 ½. At age 70 ½, however, you will HAVE to start taking taxable distributions from your IRA, 401(k), 403(b) and any other qualified account where the money has not previously been taxed. Uncle Sam mandates these required minimum distributions (RMDs) because he wants to start getting his share of the money he has not yet taxed.

The Roth IRA differs from the traditional IRA, 401(k) and other qualified accounts in that money put in investment vehicles here has already has been taxed. This Roth money has the same opportunity to grow as do the assets in a traditional IRA or 401(k). But unlike the IRA and 401(k), Roth assets are NOT taxed upon taking distributions. Check out the following chart for a quick summary of the differences between Roths and traditional IRAs.[8]

Roth IRAs vs. Traditional		
Features	Roth	Traditional
Required Minimum Distributions	No	Yes
Tax deduction in year of contributions	No	Yes
Tax-Free Income	Yes	No
Annuity income subject to social security taxes	Yes	No
Tax-Free Growth Potential	Yes	No (tax deferred only)
Tax-Free Transfer to Beneficiaries	Yes	No

Note, too, that there are no required minimum distributions on Roth IRAs. They can even be passed on to your surviving spouse or your heirs who will generally pay no taxes if they decide to take distributions from your Roth. (Talk to your tax advisor about this, as there are tax consequences depending on how the annuity passes to your non-spouse beneficiaries and how they take distributions).

---

[8] For a distribution to be taken free of income tax from a Roth IRA it has to be designated as a "qualified distribution." Qualified distributions are defined as those in which an owner first funded the Roth IRA more than five years ago and has one of the following qualifying events: reached age 59½ or older; death; disability; first-time home purchase. Non-qualified distributions can be taxed as ordinary income. Source: "Advanced Markets Q&A Book: Allianz Life Insurance Company of North America."

Moreover, assets in a Roth account do not figure in determining the tax liability on Social Security payments, as do the assets in traditional IRAs or 401(k)s.

Consider the tax advantageous nature of the Roth structure as compared to tax-deferred accounts such as traditional IRA or 401(k). Distributions from these accounts are generally taxable in the tax year in which they are taken, or when inherited by heirs. (There is a significant exception to this rule — the stretch IRA — that we will discuss later in this chapter.)

The Value of Roth IRA Conversions

The concept of Roth conversions has been around for some time. The idea here is to gradually reduce the pool of assets in tax-deferred IRAs and 401(k)s by moving that money — either a bit at a time, or in large blocks — into a more tax-advantageous Roth IRA.

To be sure, you will pay taxes — as ordinary income — in any tax year during which you move money from a tax-deferred account to a Roth account. In theory and in practicality, though, you may help yourself more over the long term by paying taxes on Roth conversions done earlier in life — in the accumulation phase of life when you are working and have income and deductions to offset the loss to taxes — instead of waiting to take required distributions at age 70½ when you likely will have only fixed income and fewer deductions to reduce the tax hit.

Keep in mind, too, that RMDs increase each year as we get older, meaning your annual tax bill could increase as well. By acting earlier in life to slowly reduce the tax-deferred pool that will eventually be subjected to taxable RMDs, as appropriate, an investor can level out his tax payments over the years instead of taking big hits all at once at age 70 ½.

The problem, as I said earlier, is that most people don't want to pay the tax on money moved from the tax-deferred pool to the Roth IRA. Even though many know they'll have to pay this tax eventually, they choose to wait until they are forced to do so.

I often find myself wishing people could get past that thinking, for they are not necessarily helping themselves by kicking the tax can down the road. I talk to a lot of people who, when they find out what they'll be paying in taxes when they take their first required distributions at age 70½, tell me they wish they had done something sooner to relieve the situation. Obviously, this strategy won't work for everyone, especially if you don't have the additional funds available to pay the taxes at the time of conversion.

Let's look at an example that illustrates this.

This mythical — but not untypical — case involves a gentleman with around $1.5 million in qualified, tax-deferred accounts. As he nears age 70, he finds he will soon have to take out almost $55,000 in taxable first-year required minimum distributions. He also learns that amount is only going to increase as he gets older, as prescribed by IRS regulations. That taxable amount, when added to his pension and Social Security income and capital gains income from investments accounts, puts him into a whole new tax world.

This is why we often talk to people about making Roth conversions — sometimes called "carve outs" — earlier in life.

Let's say the gentleman described above started making Roth carve outs at age 65. Let's say he was able to make an ambitious conversion of $100,000 a year for the next five years from his big IRA or 401(k) accounts into his Roth. Granted, he will have to pay ordinary income tax on that $100,000 he converts every year, but the money he moves into his Roth will continue to grow there without any further tax obligation or required distributions, after five years have passed since he opened the Roth. As the size of his qualified accounts decreases to $1 million after five years, this man will see a considerable reduction in his first RMD to around $36,000 with a corresponding reduced tax burden.

Uncle Sam has his hand out and he insists that you either pay him now or pay him later.

Reducing taxes in retirement is an important strategy in helping your retirement assets live longer than you do. The following example illustrates why.

I recently had a client, age 68½, who had a nice total account of nearly $2.2 million, but all of it was in IRAs or other qualified accounts. His first-year RMD coming in two years would be around $79,800, putting him in a 24 percent tax bracket. He will pay about $19,000 in taxes on that amount alone, meaning he would see only about $60,000 in after-tax dollars from his first-year RMD.

This gentleman estimated he would need around $11,600 a month to meet expenses. But, with his tax bracket skewered by the $79,800 required distribution at age 70½, he quickly saw that he would need to take about $16,000 from his accounts each month to realize the $11,600 he wanted in after-tax income. His retirement nest egg will dwindle faster, obviously, because of the higher tax burden.

I get it, I truly do, when people say they don't want to pay the tax required to do conversions from tax-deferred accounts to a Roth IRA. But Uncle Sam has his hand out and he insists that you either pay him now or pay him later.

At least you get to pick your poison as you approach retirement. You can effectively spread out your tax payments over time by reducing your pool of tax-deferred assets at an earlier age, paying taxes on the reduced amount in one bucket as you build up the volume of mostly tax-free assets in another. Or, you can wait until age 70 ½ when you have to pay the piper for the assets that have been growing tax deferred for years.

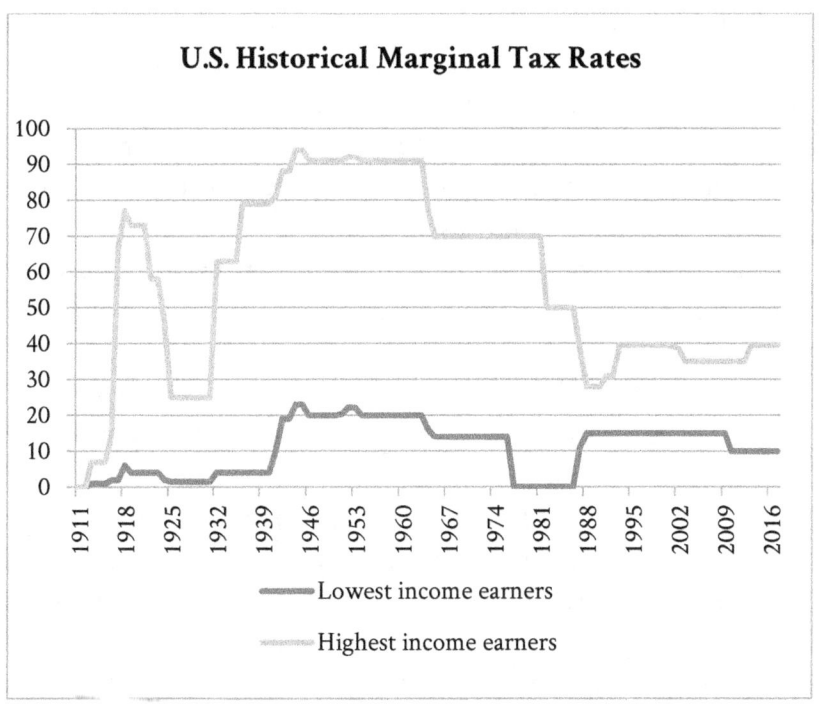

My own view on this is that we know where taxes are now, but we don't know where they will be in the future. We can make a pretty good guess, though. Our national debt only grows larger every year. How are we going to pay down that debt? I personally don't see any way of doing it without taxes going up.

Life Insurance as Leverage
in a Roth Conversion

That's why I believe if you can pay some of your impending tax obligation now, when taxes could be lower than they will be in the future (really, see the historical high-water mark for taxes if you don't believe me), it could be better for you in the long run.

That's why I believe if you can pay some of your impending tax obligation now, when taxes could be lower than they will be in the future (really, see the historical high-water mark for taxes if you don't believe me), it could be better for you in the long run.

Life insurance also can be used as a means of leveraging money taken in required minimum distributions. We're talking here about what to do with money you are required to take from your tax-deferred accounts but may not need right now to meet your retirement needs or wants.

Congratulations, by the way, if you're fortunate enough to find yourself in this situation. You don't need or especially want the RMD and would rather leave it where it is. Uncle Sam, however, has different ideas, and his is the only opinion that counts.

As mentioned briefly in the previous chapter, one option here involves taking the RMD money, paying the taxes owed from the funds taken, then applying any leftover amount you don't need into a life insurance policy that is appropriate to your particular situation. Again, policies such as the fixed indexed universal life with living benefits (as described in the previous chapter) allow you to leverage your RMD money into a death benefit for heirs, an alternative source of tax-free income for yourself or a spouse, as well as a source of funding for long-term health care expenses.

Let's look at an example of how this might work.

Remember the 65-year-old client described above who used Roth conversions over five years to reduce his $1.5 million pool of tax-deferred assets down to a more manageable $1 million? He dropped his first-year RMD at age 70½ from around $55,000 to around $36,000 after five years of making $100,000 Roth conversions.

Now, he still has RMDs to take every year on his $1 million tax-deferred pool, and he's fortunate enough not to need all that money. What's a guy to do?

Well, one option is to take that annual $36,000 RMD (the percentage of which is only going to grow every year), pay the taxes from the distribution, then take whatever is left that he doesn't need or doesn't want to make an annual life insurance premium payment.

The key here is to purchase the right life policy to accomplish the right goal.

Let's say he's able to use $18,000 yearly from his RMD to pay an annual premium on a fixed indexed universal life insurance policy. (This assumes that he is healthy enough to qualify through the underwriting process). Immediately, he has roughly a half-million tax-free dollars to leave to his surviving spouse or kids as a death benefit. He also now has an immediate long-term care benefit in that he can take 2 percent monthly from his $500,000 death benefit — or $10,000 a month — to use for long-term care, should he need it. Or, he could build cash value in that policy from which he could take tax-free loans to use as an income source if he eventually needs it.

The key here is to purchase the right life insurance policy to accomplish the right goal. Different policies are designed to do different things, be it to provide a death benefit for heirs or living benefits for the insured. Some serve a combination of all of the above. The key is to deal with an insurance professional who understands insurance and can help you find the policies that best serve you.

Stretch Out Your IRA

Let's examine one more consequence of leaving a large pool of money in your tax-deferred IRA or 401(k) accounts.

At the time of your death, the beneficiaries you have designated when setting up these qualified accounts — most likely your spouse and/or your children should your spouse precede you in death — will inherit whatever is left in your tax-deferred pools. Unfortunately, they also inherit an immediate tax obligation on that money, meaning a great deal of what they inherit goes immediately to taxes, depending on how they elect to take the funds. A spouse beneficiary, for example, can continue your IRA in his or her own name and become the new owner of the IRA, with all of the distribution options that were available to you. The ability to effectively "take over" the IRA at your death, however, won't be available to a nonspouse beneficiary and their options for how to take the money will be more limited – and therefore potentially more expensive, taxwise.

Remember, Uncle Sam has yet to get his cut of your money that has been growing tax-deferred. If he hasn't gotten it from you while you are alive, he'll get it from your heirs when you're not.

There is, however, a way to pass on even tax-deferred IRA money to your heirs in another tax-advantageous situation.

The inherited IRA, also commonly known as the "stretch IRA," allows an IRA owner to pass on to his beneficiaries his remaining qualified assets in a way that gives those assets the opportunity to continue to grow tax-deferred until the beneficiaries take taxable distributions that can be spread out over the beneficiary's life.[9] The amount of the required distribution is determined by the beneficiary's life expectancy, and — like the RMDs taken by the original IRA owner — they will increase as the beneficiary gets older.

The stretch IRA is an IRS rule as opposed to a specific investment, though the usual array of investments — stocks, bonds, annuities, fixed income — can be made under the stretch IRA umbrella.

The stretch IRA might appeal to persons hoping to help their heirs defer the tax burden they will inherit along with a large pool of taxable money. It might also appeal to parents who are reluctant to give their young adult children a large pool of money out of fear of what they might do with it.

Now, maybe it doesn't matter to you what your kids do with the money you'll leave them; after all, you won't be around to see the results. But you should know that, based on my experience, many qualified, tax-deferred accounts — whether annuities or IRAs — are liquified shortly after the death of the account owner and a surviving spouse when that couple's children inherit the taxable proceeds.

A stretch IRA can help those children avoid that immediate tax burden, even though they do not escape it completely. It can also set up a means by which they inherit your money gradually instead of in a lump sum, if that is your wish.

You can set up the stretch IRA in many ways. Sometimes they are set up as annuities, sometimes they are brokerage accounts. Banks can accept that money and put it in CDs. The inheriting child will not pay taxes until he begins taking distributions.

---

[9] If the original IRA owner dies before he begins taking RMDs at age 70½, the stretch beneficiary has the option to take a distribution in a lump sum, withdraw the entire amount in the more tax-advantageous way five years after the IRA owner's death; or take periodic distributions based on the beneficiary's life expectancy. Source: "Advanced Markets Q&A Book: Alliance Life Insurance Company of North America."

Note that these distributions will be required of the heir if the IRA owner died after age 70 ½ and was paying tax on his own required minimum distributions. But, because the RMD rate for a stretch IRA is based on the inheriting child's age as opposed to Dad's age, his RMD likely will not be as great as that Dad was having to take. If Dad had to take out $10,000 annually and pay tax on that, his children who inherit his IRA might be required to take out only $5,000 — or less — and pay taxes on that. Their RMD will increase, just as Dad's did, as they get older.

But again, the stretch IRA provides a way to stretch out tax payments as opposed to making an immediate large lump-sum payment when a large pool of taxable money is inherited at the time of the IRA owner's death.

Second-to-Die Life Insurance Policies

There also are life insurance policies are known as "second-to-die policies," meaning they pay on the death of the last surviving spouse.

Let's say the dad described previously invested half of his annual $36,000 RMD into one of these policies. By doing this, he will create anywhere from a $350,000 to $500,000 tax-free death benefit for his kids, depending on how many years he paid the annual premium. When Dad dies, the second-to-die policy doesn't pay out to Mom. But when Mom dies, the policy pays the tax-free death benefit to the children. If split between two children, a policy with a half-million-dollar death benefit pays $250,000 to each, tax free.

Now let's look at what might happen to the inheriting children if Dad elects NOT to somehow leverage the taxable IRA they will inherit.

Dad passed on a $1 million IRA split between two kids. Each inherited a half-million, and they'll probably pay a significant amount, maybe even 30-some percent, of that to the IRS in the tax year they inherit, leaving them with around $340,000.

But, if Dad invested some of his IRA money from taxable distributions either before or after he is required to take them — in a life insurance policy that built up a half million death benefit, his two kids will each inherit $250,000 tax free in addition to the IRA money. The death benefit more than makes up for what each will pay in taxes on the inherited IRA. The life insurance policy becomes, in effect, one of Dad's final gifts to his children.

Another advantage of the second-to-die policy is that if Dad is 70, say, and Mom is 65, the premium is based on her age, not his. The premium often becomes a little less expensive, again if they qualify through medical underwriting.

Why Haven't I Heard About These Options Before?

Why don't more people know about these different options?

To be brutally frank, it's often said that most people spend more time planning their vacations than they do their financial futures. They don't take the time to learn about new opportunities or how new thinking might help them down the road.

If you don't seek this information by talking to the right people — as opposed to just getting it off the internet, which can be poison — you might not learn about things that might be right for you. There are a lot of ways to get things done, but you need the right tool for the task. If George Washington had attacked that cherry tree with a spade instead of an ax, the tree would probably still be standing, and our country would have missed out on one of our greatest legends.

Which brings me back to a point I've been trying to make throughout this book.

There are ways today to achieve guarantees, cash flow and income for life without having to worry about the whims of Wall Street. Granted, these ways tend to be more conservative and may lack the potential for big reward that comes with taking big risks. But, whether you take things slow or fast, either way will get you around the track. Maybe you enjoy that stock market thing with its running and jumping all the time. Or, maybe you prefer to just circle the track without doing all that jumping – or perhaps a combination of both! You can be a hurdler if you want, or you can reduce and even eliminate the obstacles. It's your call.

> *Most people spend more time planning their vacations than they do their financial futures.*

Either way, make sure you consider all your options, getting the best information you can from the right person. Then, make sure whatever plan you put together is comfortable for you, and more importantly, that you understand it.

CHAPTER 8

Turning Assets Into Income

've been fortunate in my career to have worked with a large number of knowledgeable clients who had a good or at least a general understanding of what it takes to save and prepare for their retirement. I also feel fortunate to have assisted people who weren't as well prepared, but were still able to help themselves through some time-tested advice and planning guidance.

Over that time, I've found something of a common thread among so many of those clients, whether they did well in building a retirement nest egg or were scrambling to make up for lost time. That is, many of them know more about amassing retirement assets than they do about converting those assets to income.

Most people understand there are different phases in our lives, especially that there is a huge difference between the accumulation phase of our working years and the distribution phase that comes with retirement. The analogy often used is of a farmer planting and growing crops, then harvesting and taking those crops to market.

The transition in life from cultivation to harvest, from accumulation to distribution, isn't quite as pronounced as when a farmer first takes his combine into the field. Instead, in life there is a time some call "the financial red zone," a period five to seven years before starting retirement, where people should prepare themselves for the big transition just ahead.

This is the time you have to start thinking about what is most important in your immediate future. You're about to leave the time of your life when you could afford to take greater risks with your investment income, when you were more concerned about getting the biggest bang for your buck and had time to recover from inevitable market downturns.

> *Many [soon-to-be-retirees] know more about amassing retirement assets than they do about converting those assets into income.*

But now, as you creep closer to your target retirement date, you have to understand that, while how much you've managed to save is still important, what's even more important now is the distribution of that money. How will you stretch out whatever you've saved in your IRA, your 401(k) and other accounts in a way that will last you for perhaps 30 years or more?

Much of that will be determined by the way you take withdrawals from your various accounts.

As an aside, let me say I have no hard-and-fast rule about the best way to take retirement distributions. Everyone has different needs, different assets, different goals; no cookie-cutter approach will work for everyone, though such approaches exist.

Many financial professionals advocate the "4 percent rule" of withdrawals. It's a standard rule of thumb across the financial services industry that says you should be able to withdraw 4 percent

from your retirement accounts each year, adjusting slightly for inflation each following year, and not run out of retirement income.

*When you're nearing or in retirement,
you simply can't base a large percentage of
your retirement savings on the hope that
Wall Street will perform well.*

So, the theory goes, the growth of market-based investments
should replace at least part of what you withdraw each year. In re-
ality, that may work in good market years but, as we talked about
in previous chapters, relying solely on Wall Street-based accounts
for income during dramatic market downturns such as we saw in
2007 and 2008 can be a major drain on retirement savings. Again,
when you're nearing or in retirement, you simply can't base a large
percentage of your retirement savings on the hope that Wall Street
will perform well.

Other financial professionals advocate "dollar-cost averaging
out" as a distribution strategy to consider. This is the reverse approach to "dollar-cost averaging in," a philosophy you might have
used in building your nest egg. The idea of dollar-cost averaging in:
by investing a set amount every month, when the market is up, you
purchase fewer shares at a high price, but when the market is down,
your consistently contributed dollars purchase more shares at a low
price, which then will fatten up if and when the market rises again.
The same approach should hold true when selling assets in order to
take money out of accounts, or so the theory of dollar-cost averaging out goes. Assets you sell at lower prices one month should be
balanced out by higher prices at other times.

Personally, I often favor a system in which you make more strategic withdrawals, taking money from your better-performing accounts while leaving those experiencing a downturn untouched and waiting for a time when they perform better, when it makes sense. This is the concept of taking winnings off the table as opposed to digging deeper into your pockets in order to continue playing in the game — the goal in making sure we outlive our retirement assets.

This all brings us back to a retirement objective we've spent much of this book discussing. That is, guaranteeing a core foundation of income, a steady cash flow for yourself and your spouse. We're talking again about guaranteed monthly income to cover essential expenses; income that supplements money from your Social Security, pension and other investments; income that gives you the confidence to know you can retire confidently.

The Process of Annuitization

You already know I believe annuities provide a great way to guarantee a portion of your income. You know how I like the opportunity to compound growth in the income side of an annuity contract with an income rider, by a guaranteed interest rate rollup rate in the years before you begin taking distributions. You know I believe annuities can be an important part — a part, mind you, along with stocks, bonds, insurance, cash and other components — of a well-structured retirement plan for many.

Yet, even clients who make annuities a key piece of their retirement plans may not understand the myriad intricacies involved in converting an annuity from asset to income.

Let's spend some time here describing the traditional way of taking income from annuities through the process of annuitization. We'll then talk about using another approach — one I like very much — in which an annuitant can take income using provisions of newer contracts that give him more control over the money paid out during the distribution process.

Annuity contracts, as we noted earlier, have an accumulation phase and a distribution phase. The process of moving from one phase to another, from growing the asset to taking income from it, is called annuitization.

In the first several hundred years annuity contracts were paid out, the process of changing asset to income was essentially simple.

The annuitant (customer) told the insurance company he was ready to begin receiving payments. The company's actuaries would then apply the annuitant's age and gender to mortality tables and determine how much of the income side of the annuity contract he would receive each month for however long he elected to receive payments.

If the annuitant desired, he could receive payments for the remainder of his life. He also could set up a payment schedule for himself and a spouse over her lifetime. Among the other payout options available, he could designate a defined time period over which the insurance company would make guaranteed payments to him or to a beneficiary, should he die before the period ended. In most situations, how much he received each month was determined in part by how long he elected to receive payments. The longer he wished to be paid, the less he received each month.

Annuitization has some drawbacks, however.

Once a contract is annuitized, the insurance company controls the money. The annuitant, in turn, receives a promise that the insurance company will make regular income payments for whatever period he designates. That promise to make payments is backed by the claims-paying ability of the insurance company.

Annuitization essentially ends the accumulation (growth) phase of the contract, in most cases. The value still grows, but usually at a level so small as to be inconsequential. Moreover, once the annuitant determines how he wants to receive payments, the decision is irrevocable, set in stone, with no changes allowed.

The annuitant has any number of payment options to consider before the process is finalized. Among the more common options:

• Payment for life. The insurance company makes monthly payments until the death of the annuitant. Upon his passing, no spouse or other beneficiaries receive payment. If the annuitant lives longer than the insurance company projects him to live, he could ultimately receive more in payments than he paid in principle. If he dies shortly after he begins receiving payments, the insurance company keeps the remaining money.

• Payment for life with period certain. Like the life option above, the annuitant receives payments for the rest of his life. But he can also designate a period generally ranging from 5 to 20 years in which the insurance company makes full payments to his beneficiaries should he die before that period expires. Should he live beyond the designated period, his beneficiaries receive nothing upon his death.

• Joint and survivor life option. The insurance company provides payment for two lives. Upon the death of one, the survivor receives either a full or partial payment — depending on options selected at the time of annuitization — for the remainder of the survivor's life. No additional payments are made following the death of the surviving spouse.

• Payment for period certain. The annuitant designates a period over which the insurance company guarantees payments. If the annuitant dies before the period ends, his beneficiaries receive full payment for the remainder of the period.

• Joint and survivor with period certain. Provides payment for life for two annuitants, and to beneficiaries should both spouses pass during a designated period. The beneficiaries may elect to receive a lump-sum payment instead of periodic payments through the remainder of the period. Full payment is made to both spouses throughout the designated period, and to any surviving spouse throughout the designated period. The payment decreases for a surviving spouse after the designated period.

An Alternative to Annuitization

Annuitization remains an option on all annuity contracts, but fewer people use it today because of new annuity provisions that give customers income-taking options that don't require them to give up control of their money, as is required with annuitization.

These new options, which generally became available around 2008, are a more flexible and attractive alternative in my opinion than the annuitization options that were the only choices in years past.

Income riders — the optional provisions we discussed previously that can be added to a contract for an additional fee — now give annuitants the power to exercise more control over the income they receive from the insurance company, and to do so without annuitizing the contract. Depending on an annuitant's needs or wants, he can now activate or "trigger" income riders that allow him to take systematic withdrawals as opposed to irrevocable monthly payments.

The advantage of one such income rider — the guaranteed lifetime withdrawal benefit, which is one of several options available — provides guaranteed lifetime income even should the cash value of a contract fall to zero due to distributions taken. As part of a fixed indexed annuity, the GLWB and other riders offer the chance to build your income benefit even in times when the market is underperforming. It also offers exactly what its name suggests — a guaranteed lifetime withdrawal benefit.

Note here that the GLWB and other income riders are generally added on only at the time of an annuity purchase and are largely irrevocable.

Let's look at an example of how such a rider can work.

I have a client who held a newer annuity contract for several years before he started triggering income off the rider. He called me one day and asked, "Why am I no longer receiving 1099 statements from the insurance company? I've been getting them for several years, but now they've stopped coming."

Here's the explanation.

Let's say he started the annuity with $100,000 in principal that had already been taxed. This is called a "nonqualified" account, meaning it was financed with after-tax money. When he begins to take income, he will pay tax only on the non-principal money that has grown tax-deferred.[10]

Let's say further that after five years the income side of his annuity account has grown to $150,000 before he begins to trigger income. The first $50,000 he takes is taxable, and he will get a 1099 from the insurance company reporting this to the IRS. But after that $50,000 in deferred growth is gone, he begins to take money from the principal he paid, money for which he's already paid taxes. He pays no additional taxes on that money, and consequently receives no more 1099s.

Eventually, if he lives long enough and continues to take income from the account, the income side will eventually run out of money. But guess what happens after that?

---

[10] An annuity can be either "qualified" or "nonqualified" depending on whether it was financed with money that has yet to be taxed – a qualified account – or with after-tax dollars (nonqualified). Examples of qualified accounts are those funded with rollover money from IRAs and 401(k)s. All distributions taken from qualified plans are taxed as ordinary income. Only the interest portion of distributions taken from nonqualified plans is taxable as ordinary income.

Because this client had the guaranteed lifetime withdrawal benefit as an optional rider on his annuity, he will continue to get an income check for the rest of his life. How does this happen? Because his annuity income rider says "life," and an annuity is a contract. The contract says it will pay you for life, and life means life. If he dies before the account value reaches zero, his beneficiary inherits anything that remains in the annuity.

Different Strokes for Different Folks

I don't want to suggest here that people should never consider annuitizing their contracts. This remains a viable option for some people.

If you do opt for annuitization, however, make sure you do so only after the surrender period of your contract has expired.

Times have changed, and newer—and sometimes better—products have been developed.

Most annuities have a surrender schedule — generally between five and 10 years on today's policies — in which you will pay a sliding-scale penalty for giving up the contract in its early years. A typical surrender penalty might be 8 percent in the first year, 7 percent in the second, then decreasing to no penalty at the end of the surrender period. Most annuities give you limited access — up to 10 percent of the accumulation value as the penalty-free withdrawal amount — from the account in those early years, but you take it from the cash value, not the income value. Keep in mind, too, if you annuitize during the surrender period, in most cases you annuitize only the cash surrender value as opposed to the income, value.

Let's say you paid a $500,000 premium on an annuity that in five years has grown to at least $750,000 on the income accumulation side. The cash surrender value, based on the surrender schedule, is $450,000. In many contracts, if you annuitize the contract anytime in the surrender period, you can only annuitize the cash surrender value instead of the more lucrative cash accumulation value. You're losing money.

Please understand something here. I am NOT suggesting that annuities sold before 2008 were bad investment products. Lord knows I sold enough of them, and they did exactly what they were intended to do in providing guaranteed income.

But times have changed and newer — and sometimes better — products have been developed. Because of those improvements, it's my opinion that annuitizing a contract today is not necessarily the best choice for many consumers given the options we have with today's income riders. Why would I annuitize and turn control of my annuity asset to the insurance company if I can potentially get equal income, or even more income, while maintaining some control over that money by purchasing an income rider? Why would I want to handcuff myself by making a decision that can't be changed if my needs do? (It is important to note, however, that if you purchase an income rider and then decide to cancel contract afterwards, you will have paid for the rider without receiving any monetary gain from it, so the purchase of a rider is for those who plan to hold the annuity until they're ready to take income under the rider. It offers no benefit and actually reduces your annuity cash surrender value if you cancel the contract.)

However, the new income riders are one reason why a number of my clients over the past several years have decided to transfer older contracts into newer ones with options that don't require annuitization in order to begin taking income. Beyond that, they know today's annuities also offer the opportunity to compound interest on the income side of the ledger through guaranteed roll ups today of roughly 6 and 7 percent annually. Transfers of older contracts to newer ones can be done without penalty through a 1035 exchange or direct transfer if the contract is beyond its surrender charge schedule.

Exchanging one annuity for another one is an important decision that you need to review carefully, especially if your original annuity is still subject to surrender charges. Yet, having said that, such a transfer may be with the right move for an older annuity if it adds value to your retirement plan.

Don't be overly attracted, however, by the carrot that is the bonus. Make sure you are transferring an existing contract for the right reason as opposed to the sizzle of some bonus bucks. Keep in mind that a new surrender period starts with all new contracts, and many have a bonus recapture provision for early surrender of a new contract.

Again, the key is learning all you can and making a decision that is right for you. A good way to do that is working with a financial professional such as myself who fully understands the intricacies of annuities after years of working with them.

CHAPTER 9

Who's Working For You?

I said at the beginning of this book that I'm probably not loved by many of my colleagues in the financial services industry.

That's especially true among those selling market-based brokerage investments as they hear me ask people nearing retirement age, "Why would you even consider subjecting all or most of your retirement money to the ups-and-downs of the market when you don't have to?"

Have you gotten the impression by now that I don't give a damn about what they think?

I'm venting here, but it's hard not to do so after describing previously in this book the importance of protecting retirement money — even as we grow it — when nearing or entering retirement.

I get disgusted, frankly, when I go to industry events — and yes, I still get invitations — and listen to some financial representatives talk about how well they're living off commissions from the investment products they sell regardless of how well those investments perform. I hear some financial professionals talk about how, "I'm doing well," instead of, "My clients are doing well." This really bugs me as I think to myself, "Wow, you're really good at taking care of your people, aren't you?"

Every once in a while, I want to ask these guys, "Who are you really working for? Where are the discussions about how well our clients are doing? Where are the discussions about innovations or trends that work for the benefit of the client?" I'm sure many professionals are having such conversations, but I'm also sure I'm not hearing nearly enough of them. Is this fair to our clients? And obviously not every advisor is like this. There are a lot of very good financial representatives who do right by their client every day.

> *I can't personally talk to every one of my clients every week, or even every month. But I also can't let myself collect a paycheck for doing nothing.*

I met one guy at a convention who wanted to talk about nothing but getting a $40,000 paycheck in his mailbox every month, and he has to do almost nothing to earn it. Computers are managing the investments of his clients, and he just sits back and waits for the advisor fee checks to show up.

Now, I know I can't personally talk to every one of my clients every week, or even every month. But I also can't let myself collect a paycheck for doing nothing.

Admittedly, we have some clients with insurance portfolios that don't require a lot of maintenance, largely, in my opinion, because we set things up right and in a way they could understand. They just don't tend to have a lot of day-to-day questions. But, we also have other clients who do have a lot of questions, concerns about things they are not completely familiar with, and we must be willing to bust our butts to help them.

Then there are the representatives who, if you don't have a lot of money, don't even want to talk to you. That's bull. That $25,000 of your life savings is as important to you as a $2.5 million account is to someone else. And yet, too many times, guys in my business put limits on who they'll work with and who they won't. Company restrictions sometime dictate that. It shouldn't have to be that way, but it's probably not going to change.

Which brings me to another peeve.

While I hear plenty of talk about selling product and the compensation that comes from doing so, I don't hear nearly enough discussion about helping clients take income from those investments. More importantly, I hear even less discussion about what goes into preparing a detailed, written income strategy for retirement, something that should be essential for anyone selling a financial product for someone's retirement. You need to know how much you will get from Social Security, how much from a defined-benefit pension, and how much you might get from each of your investment assets at specific times during retirement.

The bottom line is, it's possible you may be sitting down with a guy wearing a $5,000 suit, but all that tells you is that he's making money. The question left unanswered is, is he making money for you?

Hi, I'm From Washington, and I'm Here to Help

Now, because a couple of bad apples screwed things up for everybody else, I worry that the federal government is on the verge of really messing up this industry by over-reacting to the bad actors.

As this book was being written in the spring of 2018, the Department of Labor was moving to require persons working in the financial services industry who work with retirement accounts to have fiduciary responsibilities for their clients. By definition, a fiduciary is a person or a business who holds a legal obligation to act for another under circumstances that involve trust, good faith and honesty. A fiduciary is held to a higher standard of conduct and trust exceeding that in a typical business relationship.

In short, a fiduciary has a legal obligation to put a client's interests ahead of his own.

You must understand here that a majority of people selling financial products — myself included — are not representatives of Registered Investment Advisors and therefore are not required to have a strict fiduciary relationship with their clients. People such as myself in insurance sales, as well as other broker dealers and many financial professionals operate under something called the "suitability standard" that requires us to ensure that a product is suitable for a client at the time of the recommendation

Because I've always believed it's important to have a client's best interests at heart, I never thought I needed a legal document that declared I had the obligation to do so. And yet, while the DOL's ruling has been vacated for now, that is exactly what the government may require in time.

I don't care what kind of alphabet soup somebody's got behind their name. The only thing I care about is his motivation in doing what he's doing. To me, it's always been about doing the right thing for the client, and it always will be.

I've always believed it's important to have a client's best interests at heart.

I can't begin to tell you how many people I've pushed away, or how much money I left on the table, because people came to me looking to do things that were just too crazy. They come to me looking for the world, but they can't have it. They hadn't saved enough money for retirement, so now they want to take a lot of crazy risks to make up for lost time. But they can't afford to do that this close to retirement; it's financial suicide, and I won't help them do it.

Let me give you an example. I recently dealt with a 65-year-old man who was looking to improve some things for his 94-year-old father. I looked at the assets his father had and told his son, "Look, I can do a lot of things to help you, but I can't do anything for your father that's better than what he has now." His dad had better investments than anything I could offer him, so I told him to keep his dad right where he was. I ended up passing on a $200,000 account with this guy because it wasn't the right thing to do.

That's what I mean about a financial professional's motivation being more important than any kind of credential he has.

I've always found it's best to just tell people the truth. That's why, when people sit down and talk with me, I don't feed them a line of crap. I tell them the truth, even if sometimes that isn't easy for them to hear. If they want to hear something designed only to make them feel good, they need to go somewhere else.

Don't Gamble With What You Can't Afford to Lose

Which brings us full circle back to where we began.

I repeat, the years just before or entering into retirement are NOT the time to be gambling with money you can't afford to lose. This is not like when you were younger and had time to take greater risks in the reasonable hope of getting greater rewards.

And yet, at the seminars and conventions I attend, I still hear far too many financial professionals talk about selling products that carry a risk level not appropriate for people nearing or entering retirement. I hear about far too many telling clients near or in retirement, "Don't worry about this hiccup in the market; it always come back."

Well, yeah, I know it will come back. But when? I might be dead when it comes back, and I need money to pay my bills right now!

As I said at the beginning, I'm a different kind of guy. You're not going to hear from me the same stuff you'll hear from a lot of financial professionals who place their faith on the prospect of big Wall Street returns. I'm a guy who prefers steady, consistent growth — the Little Engine that Could. That goes against a lot of conventional thinking in my business, and I'm fine with that.

I've told people this before: I'm not the guy to make you rich. I'm not going to suggest it or even imply it. But I am going to help you make the right use of the assets you have and make them work for you over the long run.

How do you know whether this approach is the right one for you?

Well, everybody has instincts, and when you talk to someone for a period of time, you usually get a feeling for what kind of person he is. My belief is that what you learn from that person has a big influence on that all-important first impression. If you come out of a meeting with someone you think you want to do business with and you haven't learned what you need to know, your instinct will probably say you're in the wrong place.

Much of preparing for retirement should be an educational process. Accordingly, I make people only one promise: You will leave my office a smarter person than when you came in. If I can teach you enough about your own money, you will make the right decision for yourself, whether that involves working with me or someone else.

You've got to feel that you've been educated, that you learned something that will help you make decisions that are right for you. It's not enough to be told, "Put your money here and be done with it."

One of my roles is to teach you what you need to know so that you make the right decision. That's what this industry should be about. If after thinking things over and making the decision about what is right for you, if you want to come back and do business with me, let's talk.

About the Author

For 24 years, J. Mark Truttman has worked hard to ensure his clients' peace of mind. He has spent time assisting hundreds of people with their estate and monetary needs, while helping others take simple and effective steps towards achieving the kind of lifestyle they desire.

Mark has spoken to hundreds of people at financial seminars and insurance sales presentations throughout Northern California. He holds the Certified Senior Advisors (CAS) professional designation; licensed with the State of California Department of Insurance under license No. 0B06466; holds the Life Underwriter's Training Council (LUTCF) designation and is a member of the Better Business Bureau. He stands committed to helping his clients make wise choices according to their personal situations, and believes his highest priority is his clients' financial confidence.

A Personal Note

A Bay Area native, Mark was born and raised in San Jose, California. He resides in Livermore with his wife Terri, and has two daughters, Jamie and Bryanne. When he is not at work, Mark enjoys fishing and the occasional hunting trip with close friends and family. He has a passion for the outdoors and is always ready for another adventure.

Contact Us

If anything in this book has resonated with you, please feel free to reach out to someone in our offices for further clarification — if we are not the right fit to help you navigate a retirement income strategy, we are happy to refer you to someone who is:

Platinum Retirement Solutions

www.platinumretirementsolutions.com
6379 Clark Ave, Suite 220
Dublin, CA 94568

Phone: 408-241-0017 | Fax: 408-241-0107
info@platinumretirementsolutions.com